SMALL WORLDS
Maps and Mapmaking

KAREN ROMANO YOUNG

SCHOLASTIC NONFICTION

Library of Congress Cataloging-in-Publication Data
Young, Karen Romano. ✪ Small worlds : maps and mapmaking / Karen Romano Young.
✪ p. cm. ✪ Includes index. ✪ 1. Cartography—Juvenile literature. 2. Cartographers—
Biography— ✪ Juvenile literature. ✪ [1. Cartography. 2. Maps. 3. Cartographers.] I. Title.
✪ GA105.6 .Y685 2002 ✪ 912—dc21 ✪ 2001020964

ISBN 0-439-09545-X

10 9 8 7 6 5 4 3 2 1   02 03 04 05 06

Printed in the U.S.A.   24
First printing, August 2002

Art Direction: Nancy Sabato ✪ Book Design: Kristen Ekeland
Composition: Josemaria Olaguera
Illustrations: Ingo Fast

All photo credits appear on page 128.

For Grandma and Granddaddy, world travelers, with love always

ACKNOWLEDGMENTS

All the interviewees: You are wonderful! Thank you.

Deborah Hopkinson, Jacqueline C. Tobin, and Raymond G. Dobard, Ph.D., for permission to report on their books

All of the kids at St. Mary School in Bethel, Connecticut, who made maps for me, especially Kathryn Ebert, Hannah Knight, Colleen McClellan, and Emily Young

Regina Weir of Green Map

John Allman

Barbara Van Achterberg

Shelley Lauzon and Daniel J. Fornari at the Woods Hole Oceanographic Institute

Dr. Julian G. Paren, Dr. D.G. Vaughan, and the British Antarctic Survey

Dr. Adam Dziewonski at Harvard University

Denis Finnin at the American Museum of Natural History

Darcy Pattison for her thoughts on fantasy maps

Ira Glass and *This American Life* for information about the work of Denis Wood and Roger Hart

Barb Nathan for the loan of her map collection

Dr. Jane Gangi for sharing Patrice Ivan's work

Mom and Dad for their traveling cameras and editorial eyes

Staci and Bill for their help and photographs

Lawrence M. Parsons and Mark Monmonier for tips, info, thoughtful reading, and response

Katie Davis and Susanna Reich for coffee and criticism

Steven Malk for help and support

Kate Waters for keeping the faith

Debra Keller and Debbie Duncan—always!

Mark, Bethany, Sam, and Emily—my world

"To give someone
directions you have to
draw a line in your mind
and then follow it
as you tell them how to go."

–Bethany, age 14

Contents

A Stranger in a Strange Land

I was flying into Chicago's enormous O'Hare Airport, and I was nervous. I had to make a connection to New Orleans. That meant finding a new gate, a new airplane. Everyone else on the plane was going somewhere different: The man beside me was headed for Mexico City; the boy across the aisle was on his way to San Francisco. There was an announcement. A voice listed all the destination cities and gave the number of the gate where each plane would be. The gate for New Orleans was K11. Well, where was this K11?

Then a flight attendant put a card in my hand. On it was a map of the terminal building where we would be landing. It was funny looking, a big place in the shape of a sideways Y. I looked out the window, waiting to land. We were flying over the airport. That's when I saw it, a building that seemed to jump out at me. From up there, I could see it was shaped like a sideways Y!

While flying, I had the same view as the one on my map, a view from above, as if I were a bird. I could see the shape of the building I was going to have to find my way around. I knew where I was. I knew where to go to find gate K11, and my feet weren't even on the ground yet. I clutched that little map like a treasure. With my map, I had big, busy, confusing O'Hare Airport in the palm of my hand.

Where am I?

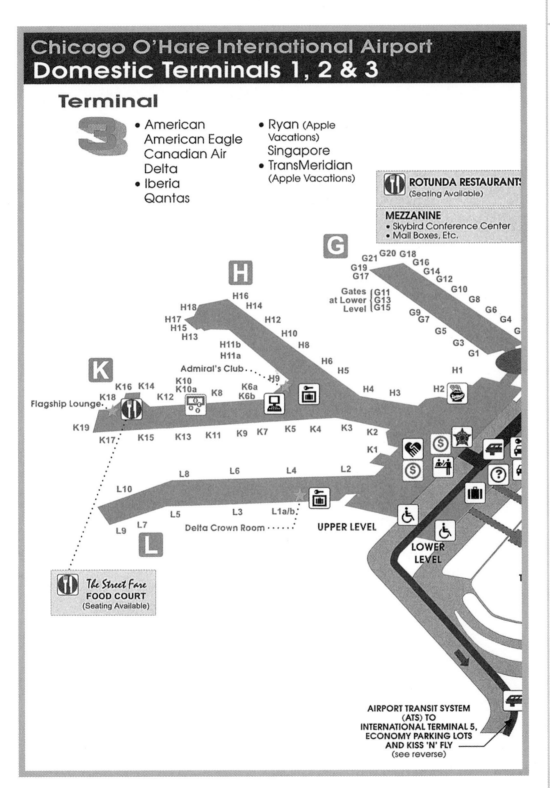

Chicago O'Hare International Airport
Domestic Terminals 1, 2 & 3

Terminal 3

- American
  American Eagle
  Canadian Air
  Delta
- Iberia
  Qantas
- Ryan (Apple Vacations)
  Singapore
- TransMeridian (Apple Vacations)

ROTUNDA RESTAURANTS
(Seating Available)

MEZZANINE
- Skybird Conference Center
- Mail Boxes, Etc.

G
G21 G20 G18
G19 G16
G17 G14
G12
Gates G11 G10
at Lower G13 G8
Level G15 G6
G9 G4
G7
G5
G3
G1

H
H16
H18 H14
H17 H12
H15
H13 H10
H11b H8
H11a
Admiral's Club H6
H9 H5
H4 H3 H2
H1

K
K16 K14 K10
K18 K10a K8 K6a
Flagship Lounge K12 K6b
K19
K17 K15 K13 K11 K9 K7 K5 K4 K3 K2
K1

L
L8 L6 L4 L2
L10
L5 L3 L1a/b
L9 L7
Delta Crown Room
UPPER LEVEL

LOWER LEVEL

The Street Fare
FOOD COURT
(Seating Available)

AIRPORT TRANSIT SYSTEM (ATS) TO INTERNATIONAL TERMINAL 5, ECONOMY PARKING LOTS AND KISS 'N' FLY (see reverse)

Oh! Chicago's O'Hare Airport Terminal 3!

CHAPTER 1

How to Make a Map

Every little map—and there are hundreds of thousands of maps—shows a world. A map can show all the space in the universe, or all that's inside a cell. This book is about maps—small worlds you can hold in your hand.

What does it mean to have a map? What can one piece of paper, one computer screen, or one globe show about a place that's much larger—or much smaller?

And what does it mean to make a map? How does a person take a place—a street, the earth, or the whole universe—and make it into something small enough for someone to hold?

The first maps were made by people who went somewhere they hadn't been before. People made maps before they could write, and, possibly, before they could speak to one another. Today, people who can't read or who don't speak the same language can still find their way using the same maps. It's a physical world, and people want to show the way physically.

Try giving someone directions without using your hands or any other part of your body, just language. Can you do it? Most people find it hard to keep from pointing, turning from side to side, drawing pictures in the air, gesturing, or drawing an actual picture—a map.

Consider this: I can give you directions to my house, and you'll know how to get there. Or I can give you a map of my neighborhood. Then not only can you get to my house, but anywhere else you need to go in the area.

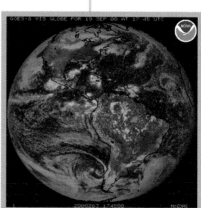

Two small worlds, one old, one new. One mapmaker used his imagination to map the world as he knew it. The other used images from a satellite that could actually take pictures of the world from afar. What story does each map tell?

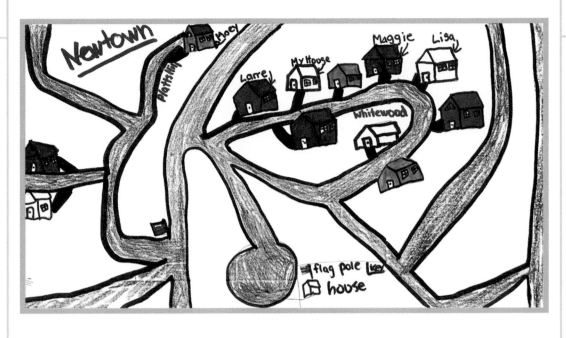

Kathryn Ebert drew this map of her world.

When someone gives you a map, it's as if they give you the place that's on it. A map helps you get a picture in your head of a place you've never visited.

The Land in Your Hand

If the mapmaker could ask the map user questions, here's what they might be:

- What do you want to do there?
- What do you need to know about the place to do what you want to do?
- What should I show you so that you'll know what you need to know?

Each map in this book had a *cartographer*, a creator who wanted to share something he or she had learned about the world. I'll begin with the most basic maps—those that show the lay of the land.

To draw a map that represents a real place, I need to start right here where I am. Here's a picture of a place I am happy to visit: the beach at Morro Bay, California. That's me, waving.

Here I am!

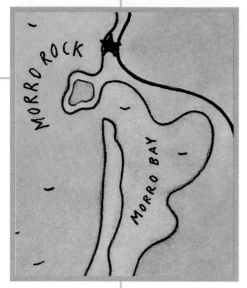

Here I am!

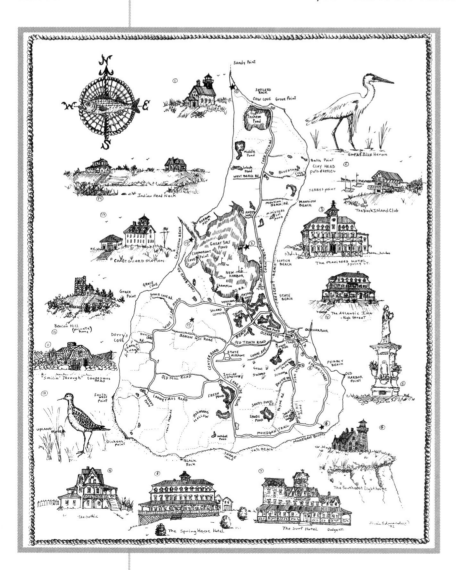

If I gave you directions to where I am standing, here's what I might say: "Get off Route 1 at the Morro Bay exit and head for the beach. I'll be on the north side of Morro Rock."

If I really wanted to help you find this exact spot, though, I'd give you a map that shows the shape of Morro Bay, the distance and direction from place to place, and my location. To get started drawing my map, I'll start with a little star. That's me. What else should I show? How much of the area around my star should my map show? That depends on how the map will be used.

If you're going to use the map to come meet me at the beach, you'll need a close-up map, one that shows the details of the place where you'll find me.

If you want to see where in Morro Bay I'm located, you'll need a bigger picture, one that shows the whole town.

To see where Morro Bay is, check out a map of California.

To see where in the country Morro Bay is, get a larger view—a map of the United States.

Other maps might show where in the world I am, or where in the solar system. A visitor from another planet who wanted to meet me on the beach could head for the right general area—southern California. He'd need a map that would let him zoom in closer if he wanted to—AAGH!—and zero in on me.

Compare this Block Island map to the Paris map on page 13. This map was drawn on a smaller scale, because the island really is too big for most visitors to walk. The map helps them figure out where to climb cliffs, take short walks, swim, bike, eat, and shop.

MAPMAKER

Jeanne Oelerich

For Jeanne Oelerich, maps are the next best thing to being in the cities she loves. Her Walking Guides began as a way to remember—and pass along—a favorite route. "People traveling in Europe are not sure what they can do or where they can go." This is especially true, she says, of cities where the dominant language is not English.

Oelerich thinks a firsthand experience helps make her maps more reliable. "I start with a basic street map, and blow it up to a size with a scale that's comfortable for walkers. I walk up and down, look at things upside down and backwards. I bring back tons of info: restaurants, museums, places where famous people lived, historic buildings. And because I have this crazy map brain, I remember where I am."

After she has created a map, she goes back to the city again to test it out. "What I say is on a street corner is on that corner," she claims. That's what makes her maps a success. "People send me e-mails and postcards telling me about the days they've spent following my maps."

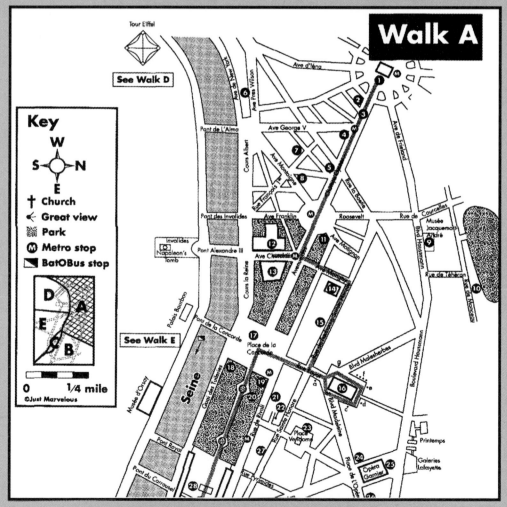

Jeanne Oelerich uses a large-scale map to share her favorite walks, such as this one, which shows Paris.

Making a Map Sandwich

A map is like a stack of layers, one showing through to the next. Each layer shows one feature of the map, such as the shape of the land; features like hills and lakes; roads, cities, airports, and highway exits; place names and other labels; and more.

Just like a sandwich, it's the ingredients that give a map its special "taste."

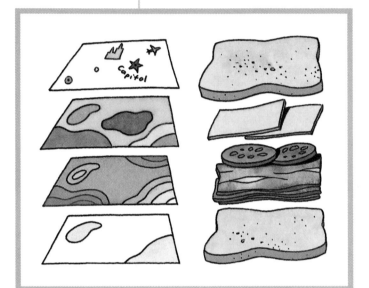

The different layers a cartographer includes are what make each map (like each sandwich) different.

Scale: How Big?

The base layer of the map is the outline of the place it shows. The first decision a cartographer makes is *scale*—how big a chunk of the world to show, and how many details about it to show.

You usually can't draw a map the size of the place you're picturing. It's just too big. You have to make everything smaller. How can you make your map show distances correctly, so that someone following it won't get lost? You scale it down. This means you make everything smaller by the same amount—10 times smaller, or 50 times smaller, or 12,000 times smaller. A mile in the real world might be represented by an inch on my small map of Morro Bay. This means that if my map left a half inch between Morro Rock and me, I'd have to walk a half mile to get to the rock.

Scale is the relationship between a distance on a map and the distance on the ground. *Large-scale* maps show a small area in lots of detail, such as a city block, a park, or a beach. They are typically used by hikers, tourists, engineers, or architects. *Small-scale* maps show a large area. They don't include as much detail as large-scale maps. For example, a world map might have a mountain range sketched in, but it won't show every single mountain.

Maps drawn to different scales zoom in on Hartford, Connecticut.

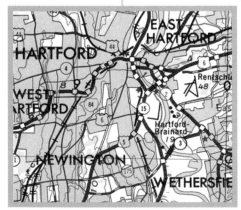

highways…1:250000

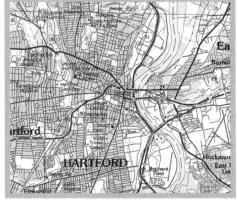

streets…1:100000

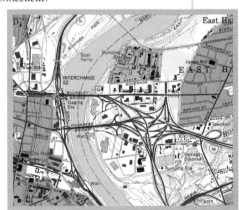

buildings…1:24000

The Language of Color: What's the Difference?

Color is a kind of language in maps. A map with *true color* shows land features. The highest mountains are usually darkest brown, plains are green, and the deepest water is the deepest shade of blue. Once you get used to the language of color a map uses, you can see what the features are at a glance.

But color can also allow another layer of information to be squeezed into a map simply and easily. Political maps use color to show where one state or country stops and another begins. Your state looks pink, yellow, or orange. Most people understand that your state isn't really pink all over; it's just the color language of political maps.

False color is another kind of map language. False color links characteristics with colors. For example, ocean maps often use false color to show water temperatures. Computers have made false color very easy for cartographers to use. By assigning a color to the temperature at each different part of the ocean, the map can be flooded with color in an instant. At a glance, you can understand water temperature differences in all of the oceans of the world. (For more about false color, see Chapter 5.)

Symbols: What's Here?

On a treasure map, the letter X marks the spot where the treasure is buried. This is an example of another map language: symbols.

Symbols can be as simple as the trail code on ski maps. If you're an expert skier, try a black diamond. If you're a beginner, look for the green circles. Intermediate? Go for the trails marked with a blue square.

Symbols may be shapes, lines, patterns, or colors for which you need a key to understand. They can also be little pictures—like icons on a computer—that are easy to figure out.

What difference does color make?

A mapmaker can choose any symbols she wants for her map. Emily Young chose these. The best symbols are easy for anyone to understand both in the key and on the map.

West Building

Main Floor

Ground Floor

This map of the National Gallery of Art in Washington, D.C., uses color to show each floor.

Location: Where?

Imagine drawing a circle around the whole earth. The most famous world circle is the equator, which runs from east to west. Travel 15 degrees north of the equator and draw another circle from east to west. Draw east–west circles all the way to the North and South poles. These lines are *latitude lines*. Now start at the North Pole and draw a line south to the South Pole. This is a *longitude line*, also called a *meridian*.

Longitude and latitude lines are divided into degrees. Degrees are divided into minutes, and minutes into seconds. Every place on the globe has a number— its position. Plotting your position is like playing a game of Battleship. Choose the right position, and you'll find the battleship. Morro Rock's global position is 35°22'10"N, 120°49'08"W. That's 35 degrees north of the equator, plus 22 minutes and 10 seconds; and 120 degrees west of the prime meridian (the 0° longitude line that passes through Greenwich, England) plus 49 minutes and 8 seconds.

(Left) Latitude lines run from east to west. They circle the globe, running parallel to one another, and never meet. They are 15 degrees apart and add up to 360 degrees, a full circle. (Right) Longitude lines run from north to south and meet at the poles. The lines are also 15 degrees apart—360 degrees all the way around. But at the equator, each degree of longitude measures 1,000 miles, while at the pole each degree measures just about nothing.

East Building

Tower Level
Upper Level
Mezzanine
Ground Level

Concourse Level

You can use a GPS (Global Positioning System) monitor to find out where you are. GPS data come from a system of satellites orbiting Earth 12,000 miles up. There are always nine GPS satellites in range of any point on the earth. They send out signals that a GPS monitor picks up. With GPS, cartographers know exactly what the position of each place is—where it is on the globe.

On a compass rose, words stand for angles. The cardinal directions are north, south, east, and west. This compass shows all the compass points cartographers use to describe directions.

Direction: Which Way?

Direction is the angle you have to travel from one place to get to another. It's important for maps to show the angles correctly. Say you made a map showing Reno, Las Vegas, and Lake Tahoe. On the ground, the direct path from place to place forms a huge triangle. On a map, the triangle would be an exact miniature of the one on the ground—with the same angles in the corners. So, if Reno is southwest of Las Vegas on the ground, it should be the same southwestern angle on the map.

Direction is something basic we expect of maps today, and a cartographer who puts north at the top helps the map user figure things out quickly. There's really no reason that north has to be up—except that it's what most people are used to.

ROAD CLASSIFICATION

Heavy-duty................. ▬▬▬▬   Light-duty................. ▬▬▬▬

Medium-duty............ ▬▬▬▬   Unimproved dirt ======

◯ Interstate Route   ⬠ U. S. Route   ◯ State Route

How large and important is a road? You can tell by comparing it to other roads on the map. How do these lines compare?

MAPMAKER
Wendy Brawer

Wendy Brawer's maps and map symbols change the way people look at their communities.

Wendy Brawer makes maps of "green sites"— places of interest to an environmentalist: wetlands, bamboo forests, sunset-watching spots, solar-energy sites, waste dumps, oil spills, and more. She created her own symbol language, inventing 100 Green Map icons.

Since Green Maps are used around the world, it's important to make sure the symbols mean the same things in different places. "At first," Brawer says, "a bowl of food was our symbol for a restaurant. But people in some places thought it looked like a bowl of bugs. A plate was just a circle; it didn't mean anything. Now we use an apple with a fork and spoon. No, you don't eat an apple that way, but as a symbol for a restaurant, this makes sense."

When you make a map, Brawer says, you decide what's important about a place. The Green Map of Copenhagen, Denmark, includes a symbol for shops where you can get your bike repaired for free. And the Kyoto, Japan, map has a symbol that stands for firefly-watching zones. Kids in Calgary, Alberta, put cloud-watching sites on their map.

What's it like to make a Green Map of your own neighborhood? See page 38 for more.

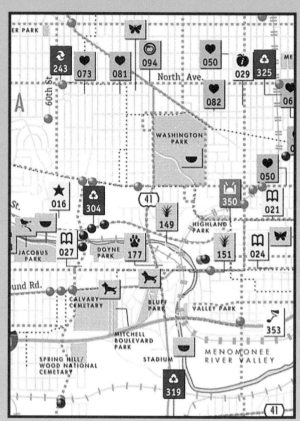

Milwaukee Green Mappers create symbols to show everything from firefly-watching zones to farmers' markets.

Putting a Map to Work

1. Find a Reference Point

Take a look at the map on page 19. Can you identify the place it shows? Now turn the page and look at the map that almost matches this one—except for one label. Knowing one point on a map—one place—gives you a link to the real world.

Finding a point like this—it's called a *reference point*—is key to translating the information on a map to what you see "on the ground."

2. Get Oriented

Next, you have to get oriented. Go to the Orient? Not exactly, but close. The Orient is another name for Asia, which is also called the Far East. The word *orient* comes from people who lived in the West. If they could figure out which way was east, then they could figure out which way to go to reach their destination. In ancient times, maps even had East at the top, to help people get oriented. If you faced the rising sun, and held the map right side up, you could easily figure out which way to turn to reach your destination.

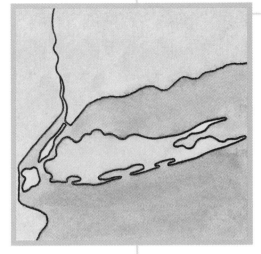

Where is this? Turn the page to find out!

3. Head in the Right Direction

Using a compass is a more precise way to figure out direction than using the sun, which doesn't always rise exactly in the east, and which isn't always rising, anyway. If I'm standing on Morro Beach, my compass points north, and the markings around the compass show me the other directions I might take. My map shows that I should go southwest to get to Morro Rock. Even if it's dark or foggy, I'll eventually bump into Morro Rock.

By finding a point of reference, getting oriented correctly, and moving off in the right direction, you'll get where you need to go. Right? Right, as long as your mapmaker gave you the information you need.

Putting It All Together

My mother's car has an amazing feature: a navigator. This computer uses GPS to keep track of where Mom is. When she types in my address, the navigator won't just show her a map, it'll direct her through every step of the route. Mom doesn't even have to look at it. The computer talks. "Turn onto the New Jersey Turnpike," it tells her, and before she knows it, she's at my door.

How on Earth does it work? (And what does Mom do if it doesn't?)

First, the computer uses GPS to figure out where Mom is. She types in her destination, and the computer computes the GP of that. Then it finds the most direct route for Mom to take to get from place to place. The computer has a database

GPS helps my mom know where she is and where she's going.

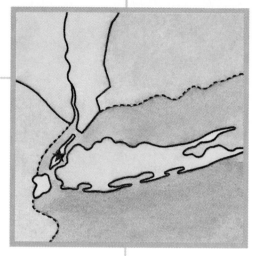

New York, New York!

that links addresses with global positions, and that contains all the roads. What's more, Mom's navigator can find businesses—like hotels, restaurants, and gas stations—along her route. The database holds layers and layers of information that could be combined to make exactly the map Mom wants.

A cartographer includes different things—and different layers—depending on how the map will be used. Put a layer of information about a place on top of a map that shows the geography of a place, and you can suddenly "read" a whole new story as you read the new map you've created.

Here's an example of a custom-made map that I made for myself for a specific purpose: so dogs wouldn't chase me while I was jogging (I hate that!). I started with a basic street map of my area. It's really a three-layer map: my area + roads + dogs. My dog information comes from a chart I made showing which streets have dogs.

Long Meadow Lane	Sunrise Hill	Shelley Road	Rockwell Road	Whippoorwill Lane
Yogi	Franky	Willow	Trooper	Sellie
Toby	Elsa		Bruno	
Freckles				

My data shows where dogs live in my neighborhood.

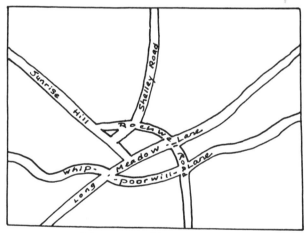

This is my neighborhood.

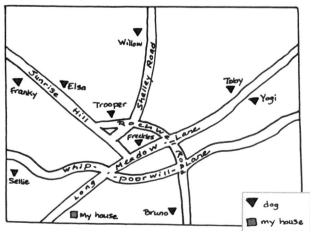

The triangles show where the dogs live.

▼ dog
■ my house

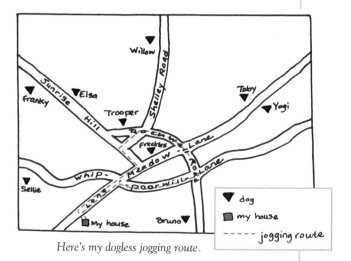

Here's my dogless jogging route.

▼ dog
■ my house
----- jogging route

Layers of Discovery

Special maps have special layers, such as population (how many people live in the place), geology (what's going on underground), biology (what lives there), weather (where tornados are likely), businesses (where the vegetarian restaurants are), recreation (where to camp), and so on. There are maps for all of these things and many more.

Layers have let people use maps to make discoveries throughout history. In 1854, Dr. John Snow, a London doctor, treated an epidemic of cholera, a fatal disease that is spread through contaminated water. On a map of London, he kept track of the households where someone had cholera, drawing a dot for every case. Then he drew the pumps where Londoners got their water. One pump was at the center of the largest group of dots. This map with two layers, one geographical (the land) and one informational (the dots and pumps), helped stop the cholera epidemic.

These days, maps that match up information with places are made on computers. Where does all the information on maps come from? Someone goes out and finds it, like Dr. Snow. His set of data included the households with cholera and the location of the pumps. Snow gathered his data by checking records and asking questions.

Today's cartographers use their own data, like Snow, plus GIS (Geographical Information Systems), big databases with information about different places. Cartographers can use GIS to find a basic map outline, and then use their computers to stack new data with old to create new maps on the spot. With the click of a button, they can make maps that show the precise information a user is looking for.

The Map Deli: Ingredients to Go

No map can show you everything about a place. Not all information about a place can be put on one piece of paper. For maps to communicate, they focus on showing a limited number of things.

Your moves—what you're going to do in a place—determine the kind of map you need. Take Disneyland. Say you were going to visit and go on the rides. To plan your day, you'd need a tourist map—one that shows what rides there are and how to get from one to another.

Say you were a plumber working on a water leak in the ride "20,000 Leagues Under the Sea." A map that showed the inner workings of Disneyland might help.

What if you were a pilot making an emergency landing near Disneyland?

MAPS MAKE THE DIFFERENCE

Alice Hudson

Alice Hudson is Chief of the Map Division of the New York Public Library—the library with the two big lions outside and thousands of maps inside. "My interest in maps probably comes from early on. My grandmother sent a subscription to *National Geographic* to us. My sister and I used to have a searching game with the maps. One of us would look for the smallest, weirdest, most out-of-the-way location, and the other had to try to find out what tiny part of China or Yugoslavia, or wherever, it was."

Now Hudson is in charge of one of the largest and most important map collections in the United States. Not only does she lead decisions in what maps to purchase for the collection, she works with people who are donating maps, and helps library patrons answer questions through maps.

"'I'm sure you can't help me,' people will come in and say. They've already tried the almanac or the dictionary or the encyclopedia—but 90 percent of the time we can find their answers through maps." One might want to know the location of a village in Eastern Europe where her grandparents lived before immigrating. Another wonders if there's a river or stream under his house, because he can hear water in the basement. A novelist needs to learn the traffic patterns in the city in the time when her novel is set. Was Fifth Avenue a one-way street yet?

"Two different young African-American women have come looking for the locations of small towns in the South where family members have said they lived during the Civil War. They have no proof, just a note in a family Bible or a story passed down. We'll find the location and prove together that the family history is real. There are tears! A map is a very strong emotional tool." Maps are emotional and deeply personal.

Still, people believe that anything that's on a map is true. But there is no map that's neutral. Every map has a point of view. The mapmaker shows his point of view by what he puts on or leaves off the map. When you make a map, you leave off a lot of reality.

Maps with not enough information may be spread around on purpose during wartime, Hudson says, mentioning a map of the East Coast of the American colonies that helped sink enemy ships during the Revolutionary War. "It's amazing to have an historical map in front of you. You can see the quality of the paper, the different colors, even the handwriting someone put on the back," Hudson says.

These days you can get on the Internet and find pictures of many of the historical maps held by the New York Public Library and other great map collectors, including the Library of Congress, the British Library, and many, many more.

Alice Hudson is Chief of the Map Division of the New York Public Library—the library with the lions in front.

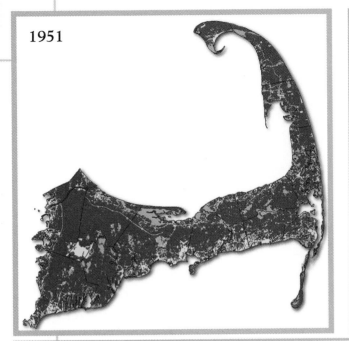

1951

1990

| NATURAL AND AGRICULTURAL | DEVELOPED | WATER AND WETLANDS |

A GIS was used to make this map that shows how land use in Cape Cod, Massachusetts, changed over 39 years.

Stars lead to stars on this map of Hollywood celebrities' homes.

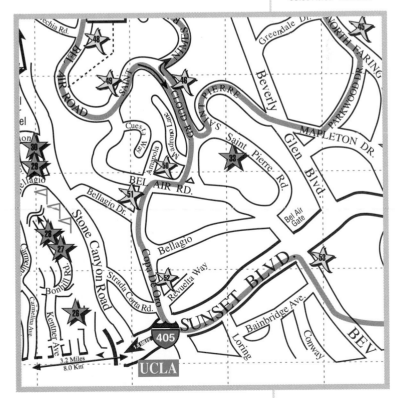

You'd need a map that showed the shape of the land, so you could find a flat, open space away from buildings. And it would help if the distances on the map matched those on the ground. Then you could be sure your "runway" was long enough for you to land on.

The kind of map you create depends on the information that you layer into it. GIS databases provide an infinite number of layers that any map could have: the base map, roads, land use, wildlife, even what's under the surface of the earth. Geographic Information System programs hold information about everything from population size and forest-fire hot spots to murder sites and the number of telephones every household has. The program links each piece of information with a point on the map to create a layer. Depending on what information you need, you can choose different layers to make thousands of different maps of the same area. With a few clicks anyone—not just professional cartographers—can create maps that exactly meet their needs.

In New York City, police were investigating a series of crimes. They put the locations of the crimes into their database, and they came out as symbols on the map showing where the crimes had taken place. The next layer showed places where a local gang hung out. When the layers were put together, like a sandwich

MAPMAKER

Staci Romano

Staci Romano mapped the Transamerica Pyramid.

Staci Romano is an interior architect who drew the emergency route maps for the Transamerica Pyramid in San Francisco. You can find an emergency escape map on the wall of every floor of most public buildings. Each map has just three layers: the outline of a building, features such as rooms and stairways, and arrows pointing the way out.

Q. What do you have to think about when you draw an emergency map?

A. I had to look at the escape route from the point of view of every person in the building and imagine what they would need to get from looking at the map. The first thing I think about is how each person should exit.

Q. What special challenge did the Transamerica Pyramid present?

A. The Transamerica building has a distinctive shape. It widens to the fifth floor. Then every floor above the fifth floor gets smaller and smaller. So each map had to be sized slightly differently.

Q. How do you make emergency maps the simplest, clearest maps for people to follow?

A. It has to be easy to read. The map has only room numbers, hallways, stairways, and things you'd need to find if there was a fire: stand pipes, fire extinguishers, pull stations, and fire hoses. There are simple symbols like a square or a circle to illustrate where things are. There's a color code, too, determined by the fire department of the city. According to the San Francisco Fire Code, the exit arrows must be green because that's the way you want people to go. Red is used for the fire equipment.

of clear plastic sheets, it showed the police new information: that the crimes took place close to the gang hangouts.

Businesses use GIS to decide where to put new stores. For instance, a company that sells car parts and services can use GIS to find places with lots of cars, and put stores there.

Geographic Information System is a way of getting dull sets of statistics into a form that people can look at and understand instantly. Maps like this have been a long time coming.

People in a small Connecticut town were building a shooting range. They didn't think the noise would bother anyone. But a neighbor took a map of the town and made a dot where the shooting range would be. Then he added house symbols in the area around the range. He figured out how far the sound of the shots would travel. He drew a ring on his map at the sound limit. People in all of the houses inside the ring would hear the shots. The number of houses inside the ring was enough to get a lot of attention for the neighbors' protest—and change the way people thought of the shooting range.

MAPS MAKE THE DIFFERENCE

The Marin County Fire Department

The Marin County Fire Department, in northern California, uses GPS and GIS to fight forest fires. Here's how it works:

1. Helicopters fly over the fire and use GPS to find out precisely where and how big the fire is.
2. The helicopters land at the fire scenes. Firefighters download the GPS information into computers.
3. The GPS information adds to a GIS database of the area. The GIS shows the firefighters who owns the area, what buildings, people, animals, and types of land are there. Another part of the database holds a road map so firefighters can choose a route to the fire.
4. Maps are printed out at the scene of the fire. Each firefighter gets his own map. They get the land in their hands—the land they're trying to save.

"GIS gives us a better chance of coming up with a good strategy for fighting the fire," says Tim Walsh, who makes the new fire map technology work for Marin County. "In the past, we'd sketch the fire on top of a normal topographic map and duplicate it. Now we can focus and bring much more detail into the map."

CHAPTER 2

Explore the Unknown, Make It Your Own

In the 1970s, Roger Hart mapped a Vermont town using information that came mostly from walks he took with kids. Hart found out that almost every child had a secret place. He learned what parts of town kids were eager to explore or were afraid of (such as the woods). He found that kids were often eager to explore the places they were afraid of. He also asked the parents which places they were afraid for their children to go, such as areas near water or busy roads, and put them all on the same map. A map of fears? In a way, maps have always acted as mirrors of people's attitudes and feelings about places.

Places are important. If you don't think so, take a look at the people around you. How many are wearing T-shirts or fleeces or hats with the names of places? When people go somewhere, they come back wanting to tell their friends where they've been. Long, long before you could buy a T-shirt from Moose Jaw or Bondi Beach or the McMurdo Base at Antarctica, people were sharing their travels with others through maps. Maps showed where they'd been, what they'd found, how they got there, and how they felt about the place. Was it strange? beautiful? scary? full of riches? The map was the end of the story of one person's journey—and the start of someone else's.

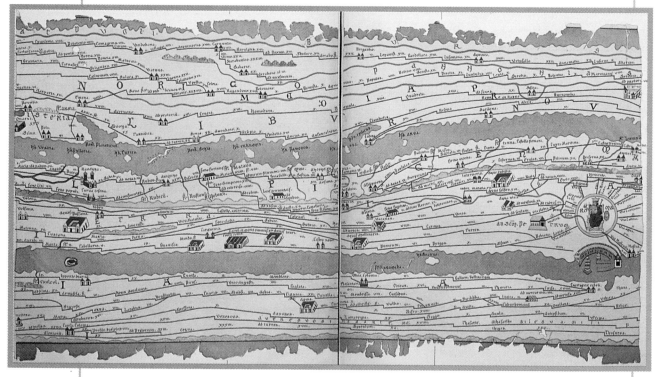

Third century A.D. *Early road maps showed routes but didn't reflect the lay of the land. This is a section of the Peutinger Table, which showed the military roads of the Roman Empire.*

In the early 2000s, Hart plans to return to the Vermont town to remap it. Now the kids he interviewed in the 1970s are the parents. Hart thinks that kids are no longer as free to wander; parents worry more about what might happen to them if they "go too far."

The word *explore* is just one letter away from the word *explode*. Nowadays people have to go pretty far—to outer space or the bottom of the ocean—to find a place where nobody has been. To ancient people, traveling 1,000 miles was like traveling to another planet today. But they traveled anyway. Is it more dangerous to explore today than it was way back when saber-toothed tigers might roam the woods near your cave? Exploration—and mapping—may just be built into humans, and nothing can change that. Since the first humans looked toward the horizon and wondered what was over there—just beyond their view—exploring (exploding your experience from the known area into the unknown) has been part of the way people learn. And mapping has followed right behind.

That Land Over There

People of almost every time and culture made maps of the land close to them— and the lands they explored. Maps helped determine what could be found in those lands and who could use the land.

Laying down boundaries was the purpose of the earliest map that we know about. A land map drawn on a cave wall in Turkey in 6500 B.C. was used to show property lines. Ownership was power, and the way to prove you owned land was to show it on a map. When disagreements about land use arose, you could refer to the map and settle the problem.

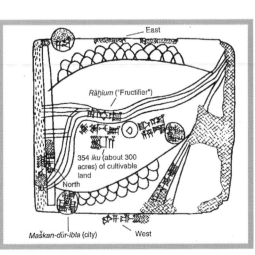

East

Rāhium ("Fructifier")

354 *iku* (about 300 acres) of cultivable land

North

Maškan-dūr-ibla (city)   West

2200 B.C.
A map from Mesopotamia (Iraq, today) showed one family's estate etched on clay.

27

MAPMAKERS

Redstone Studios

This map shows the travels of the Keller family when they visited China to adopt their daughter, Xiaoling.

Julie Ruff and Connie Brown, artists who own Redstone Studios in Millwood, New York, make personal maps for people. Personal maps show the love a person can have for a place—and the way a place can give a person "roots." Ruff and Brown use a client's travel maps, souvenirs, writing, and memories to show what's important about a place for them.

JULIE: We started when Connie took a trip through the Pyrenées mountains (along the border of France and Spain). Every night she traced the day's route on her map. Back home, she painted a map for herself showing her journey. We realized, this is very cool. We got very excited about it.

So Redstone Studios began the business of making maps for people. The artists have created maps showing a family who are very close, but live all over the world. They've done marriages, biographies, adventures like sailing journeys, and marathon races. But one of their favorite maps is the one they did for the Keller family of Bedford, New York, after they adopted a little girl, Xiaoling, from China. The map shows Xiaoling's birthplace, the Kellers' journey to bring her home, the tour of China that they made together, and something else: a list of "Sisters in Faith"—other children born in her area and adopted at the same time.

LINDSAY KELLER: When I came back from China I knew I wanted a very special way to document our journey. This map is a wonderful treasure to give to Xiaoling. In the middle is her chop, the Chinese character of her name, which means "laughing spirit." This map is about Xiaoling.

CONNIE: Lindsay brought us the things that she carried with her in China: a jade Buddha, a Chinese kite. We unite the map with the place by using the colors and designs you associate with that place.

LINDSAY: The borders came from the edges of the rice bowls we bought in China, and the wave design above her chop is from the kites we brought back.

JULIE: Making a map is like keeping a visual diary. Instead of writing, you look at your map and see a trip or a place that makes you happy.

CONNIE: People have e-mailed us their life stories. Our significant experiences always take place geographically. A map is how you show that.

LINDSAY: Life is a journey. Maps document those journeys. They are our history, and they're meant to be passed down. It's the way we look at our past and our future.

The Keller family kids

Cave maps, parchment maps, woven maps, and paper maps have something in common besides ownership, food, and fantasy. They're flat. Flat maps work because they reflect the flat land that people could imagine and hold in their minds.

Didn't people realize that the earth was round? Yes, they did. Long before Columbus tried sailing west to get to the East, people knew we lived on a sphere. But many cared less about showing how things really were than about showing what was where and whose was whose.

Before you visit a place or see a map of it, it's just a big blob in your mind. It's just *that land over there*. Sometimes, even when you've been to a place, you don't have a clear idea of its position in the world. Which way was the river, you might ask yourself: north or south? What mountains were those? Seeing a map of a place helps you understand it. And mapping a place changes how people think of it—how to travel through it, what it can be used for, and who it belongs to. Want to own the world? Make a map of it.

Showing the Way

As soon as people began traveling to trade their livestock and crops, as well as things they made, road maps were drawn to show the ways. In Asia, Europe, and Africa, maps showed trade routes across land. Trade led people to their boats, too—and to the first maps of the ways across the Indian Ocean, the Pacific Ocean, and, eventually, the Atlantic. But early maps might just as well have been called gaps. It would be up to explorers—people "exploding" out of their boundaries into the unknown—to fill in the gaps to give us a complete world view.

Cultures that built roads, bridges, aqueducts, dams, and dikes got involved in mapmaking, too. Control over the water and the roads was important to them. Mapping was a good way to make sure they controlled the entire place. For this reason, Julius Caesar ordered the Roman Empire to be mapped. As time went on, countries that were advanced in engineering—especially China, Italy, the Netherlands, and England—became great mapmaking cultures, too.

At the beginning of the first millennium, the best mappers were the people with the most information. So for many years, the best maps were created by Greek, Chinese, and Arab cartographers. In about A.D. 150, a Greek, Claudius Ptolemy, drew a flat map of the round world that included the curve of the earth. This map, and the descriptions of it that Ptolemy wrote in his *Geography*, earned him the nickname "Father of Geography." It was Ptolemy who first placed North at the top of a map, included latitude and longitude lines, and drew the earth's circumference to scale—even though his guess of 18,000 miles around was only three-fourths the earth's actual size.

Ptolemy's work was kept in the famous library that Alexander the Great had built in the city he named after himself, Alexandria, Egypt. In A.D. 391 the library—and the books inside—burned. Early Christians, who believed that scientific study and writing went against God, set the fire. Instead of maps that represented the physical world, they drew a religious world, with Jerusalem, the holy city, at the center. European maps of the next thousand years often included the land of religious leader Prester John, the evil lands of Gog and Magog, and other imaginary things designed to encourage Christians to stay put. They included drawings and warnings of evil that might befall those who explored too far. Sea monsters lurked in the waves of seas. Some maps included cautions: *Terra Incognita* (the Unknown Land) or—even scarier—*Here Dragons Be.* Unless you had a death wish, you stayed in familiar territory.

Terra Incognita

Meanwhile, people in some of the "unknown lands" were making progress in their own explorations. From about A.D. 800 through 1000, Vikings from northern Europe made many expeditions to North America, Iceland, and Greenland. They left behind carvings, tools, and even small settlements. Without a map showing their routes, however, historians have had trouble proving the Vikings' accomplishments. Cartographers today still argue about whether the Vinland Map, which shows an A.D. 986 voyage, is for real.

You can't argue with the maps of al-Idrisi, a 12th-century traveler and geographer who mapped the trade routes between Arabia, his homeland, and India. Arab merchants were on the move bringing spices and silks from Asia across the Indian Ocean by boat, through the Red Sea, and on to the Mediterranean.

Some say the greatest traveler of all time was another Arab, Ibn Battuta, who set off in 1325 on a 74,400-mile tour of the known world, crossing 45 countries,

A.D. 600
In the Middle Ages, people's worldview came from religion, not from scientific exploring or facts. Mappae mundi (maps of the world) included imaginary lands from legends. This one shows a wall around the evil legendary armies of Gog and Magog.

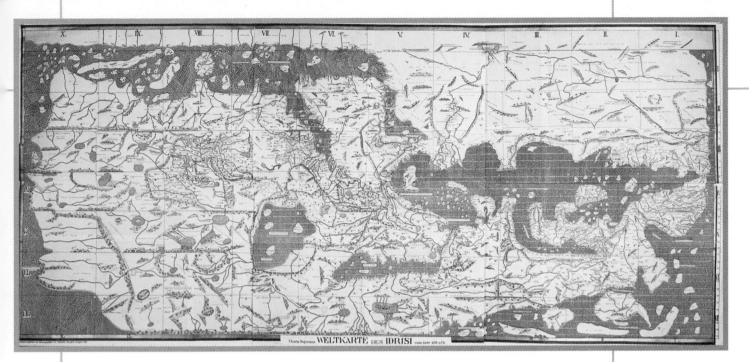

Charta Rogeriana WELTKARTE DES IDRISI vom Jahr 1154 n.Ch.

A.D. 1154
Arabs held the trade routes to India—and the maps that went with them. Al-Idrisi made this one.

including Africa and Asia. If he has a rival, it might be the Chinese admiral Cheng Ho, whose fleet of huge ships explored every land bordering the Indian Ocean from 1405 to 1433. Cheng's ships sailed around Africa's Cape of Good Hope from east to west, long before the European explorers got there from the west.

Meanwhile, things were slowly changing in Europe. From 1095 to 1271, Muslims and Christians fought for possession of Jerusalem. Now many Christians hit the road, traveling from Europe to Jerusalem to fight in the Crusades against the Muslims. New travels meant new maps, but realistic maps were still few. And now there was something else that Europeans wanted: spices.

In 1271, Marco Polo set out from Venice across central Europe to China. For 25 years, he worked for Kublai Khan, the Chinese emperor whose lands extended from what is now Hungary to the Pacific Ocean. When Polo returned home, he published his memoirs. *The Travels of Marco Polo* fed people's imaginations—and added to their maps. Christian missionaries now traveled to China as well, spreading the word of Christ. Their maps of the empire drew on the detailed maps the Chinese had of their own land.

Marco Polo helped introduce Europeans to precious gems, silks, and spices, which had uses for medicine, cooking, preserving food, and even as deodorants. These goods came to Europe through Italian merchants who bought them from traders on the other side of the Mediterranean, who carried them over Asia and eastern Europe. The result was that spices were more precious than money—and were sometimes even used instead of money. Europeans wanted to find their own way to get hold of the goods.

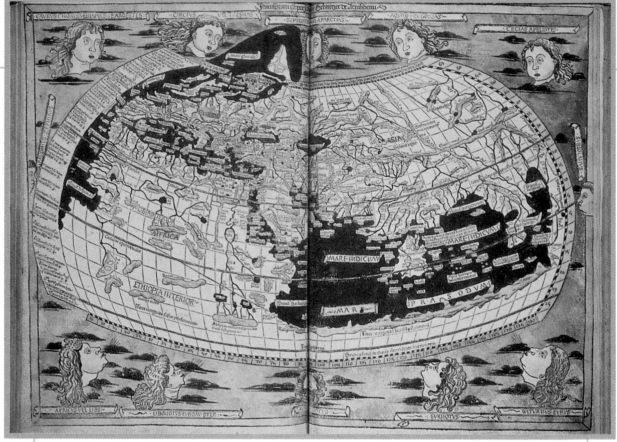

A.D. 150
Ptolemy's map was lost to history, but his book was found in the 1400s. Mapmakers used the information in the book to make "new" world maps.

The ocean—that was the ticket! In 1406, a copy of Ptolemy's *Geography* was found. The map remained lost, but Ptolemy's book was used to draw up a new map based on his specifications. If the world was round, as Ptolemy said, there ought to be a way to sail to the places where the spice trees grew. England, Portugal, Spain, France, and the Netherlands sent out explorers who headed south to Africa and west to what they thought was Asia, but was really the Americas.

What these explorers found would have been no surprise to the natives of the lands they visited, and it wasn't news to explorers from other worlds. But the bits and pieces of information they brought home were quickly put into new maps. The mapmaking effort was the most important thing that set the European explorers apart. Their explorations became fresh data for cartographers who could mass-produce their maps on the newly invented printing press. Through these maps, the word spread fast about Africa, North America, and South America. For the first time, maps of the whole world were available. Yes, these maps were the most complete to date. Yes, they were still full of problems. Some of these problems would be solved hundreds of years in the future by new technology. Some still trouble mapmakers today. And, just like today, there were some people who just wouldn't carry a map.

MAPS MAKE THE DIFFERENCE

Quilts and the Underground Railroad

You're probably aware that in the United States, slaves were not allowed to learn to read. But did you know they weren't allowed access to maps? Denying maps, directions, methods of navigation, and even place names to slaves was one of the biggest ways slave owners exercised their power. But they couldn't stop slaves from climbing aboard the Underground Railroad, a system of "stations" or safe houses that led to freedom.

Those who made it often sent back messages in songs, stories, and word of mouth. Often, the words were coded so that eavesdroppers wouldn't guess their meaning. And sometimes the code came in the patterns of homemade quilts.

In their book, *Hidden in Plain View,* Jacqueline L. Tobin and Raymond G. Dobard describe the quilt code Mrs. Ozella McDaniel Williams' family used to help one another escape to Canada on the Underground Railroad. Quilts with specific patterns, ten in all, would be hung on a rail as a signal.

A quilt with the Monkey Wrench pattern came first. It meant, "Get ready to travel." Next would come the Wagon Wheel: "Pack the wagon." Sometimes packing the wagon meant hiding inside the false bottom of a wagon. Bear's Paw meant that fleeing slaves should follow the bear's trail through the Appalachian Mountains to the Crossroads (another pattern), which was Cleveland, Ohio. A Drunkard's Path quilt indicated that a zigzag path was best for someone

Mrs. Ozella McDaniel Williams holds a Bear's Paw quilt. Was the pattern a signal to slaves preparing to escape?

who didn't want to be followed. The Star pattern gave directions to follow the stars north to Canada. Tumbling Blocks—the last pattern—said it was time to go. Slaves "read" the different messages, and when Tumbling Blocks appeared, they already knew the plan.

"The story of the Quilt Code was passed down orally—person to person—in the Williams' family since the days of slavery," Tobin says. "The whole code has never been found anywhere else." But Tobin and Dobard have found clues that certain patterns were used in similar ways in other areas. Even Frederick Douglass, an important "conductor" on the Underground Railroad, was found to have a Monkey Wrench quilt on his bed. To some people, the Monkey Wrench quilt might have meant to look for a key or "tool" person—someone like Douglass.

Deborah Hopkinson heard the story of another quilt maker/mapmaker, Elizabeth Scott, as she talked about "plantation quilts." These homey-looking hand-sewn pictures of the plantations—like the one in Hopkinson's picture book, *Sweet Clara and the Freedom Quilt*—might have shown all the areas of the plantation, including the best place to slip off the plantation grounds.

This map shows some of the routes on the Underground Railroad, which had no trains. Slaves followed these tracks north to freedom.

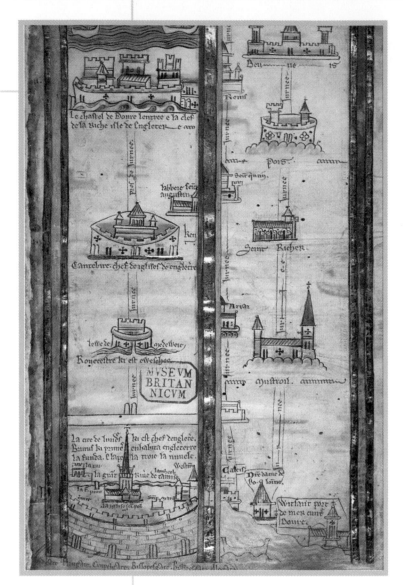

A.D. 1200s
Made of a long strip of parchment (animal skin), Matthew Paris' map of the route from England to Italy could be rolled up for easy carrying.

The Age of Discovery

No sonar, no radar, no GPS: Imagine going off on a trip—from Italy to China, from Spain to the Caribbean, or all the way around the world—and not even taking a map. That's what the three most famous explorers did. Marco Polo, Christopher Columbus, and Ferdinand Magellan took off with their eyes on the prize and no maps in their hands. Two of them lived to tell the tale. All of them "discovered" new places and brought back information that added greatly to the world's maps. For more on Columbus and Magellan (who didn't make it back alive), see Chapter 3.

The great Age of Discovery began before Columbus' time and continued until nearly 1900. It was all about being in charge not just of maps, but also of nature, resources, and treasures, which included gold, spices, and people. Again and again, natives of newly explored places were pushed out, killed, even enslaved. How did the explorers and those who came after them justify their actions? Many thought they were truly more intelligent than the natives, or that their white skin made them superior. Others wanted to bring the Christian religion to those who had never heard of Jesus Christ. But many were part of a culture of conquest. They thought it was fair for the strongest people to take over.

A saying goes: "The one with the tools makes the rules." The European explorers had guns, ships, telescopes, compasses, and more. Before long, they had maps. When I was in fourth grade, I learned about the Age of Discovery. We studied only the English, Portuguese, Dutch, French, and Spanish who "discovered" new lands and new people and came home to tell the tale. Didn't other countries send out explorers? Every other country *did*. And many of them even shared their findings by mapping them.

What made the difference? Why did we study some explorers but not others? These questions have several answers. One is that Europeans were the first to develop the printing press about the same time as the European explorers were making their voyages. Cartographers used the press to create map after map based on the voyages of Europeans, whether the information they brought home was right or wrong.

Another answer is that most American culture—history, literature, music, art, and way of life—is based on European culture. We tell the stories the Europeans told, especially when it came to how North America was colonized and new people (including ancestors of everyone but the native tribes) arrived. But the most important answer is the reason some of the first maps were drawn: ownership.

Yes, the explorers set out to find the way to India and China, which had the goods Europeans wanted. But what they found along the way were the Americas. The Americas were a gold mine. They were a silver mine. They were a copper mine. They had fields for farming, woods for lumber, animals for furs, fish galore, and land aplenty. And the Europeans claimed them for their own. This wasn't true just in the Americas. As Europeans explored and mapped, they claimed land all over the world, and even made slaves of the people who were there first.

Staking a Claim

Prince Henry the Navigator, of Portugal, made his first voyage to Africa in 1421. To Europeans, Africa was one of those big blobs on the horizon. Even Ptolemy didn't know where it ended. During the next 40 years, Prince Henry sailed and mapped 2,000 miles of the Atlantic coast of Africa. He never found the end of the blob. He really didn't know much about Africa except for what he saw. But he saw fit to start the African slave trade, forcing hundreds of Africans onto his boats and carrying them back to Europe for sale.

Other Portuguese explorers picked up where Prince Henry left off and added thousands of miles to the maps of Africa. Bartholomew Diaz sailed around the Cape of Storms, which was renamed Cape of Good Hope by mapmakers to make it more appealing to sailors. By 1502, Vasco da Gama made the voyage across the Indian Ocean to the trade port of Calicut, proving that Europeans could bypass the land routes.

A European map of this time shows only the coastline of Africa. The author Jonathan Swift made fun of such mapmakers, who used the places they didn't know anything about as spots for illustrations. He said they "drew elephants, for want of towns." Eventually, Dr. David Livingstone and other European explorers made names for themselves by traveling through and mapping Africa's so-called dark interior. Didn't the Africans know what was there? Sure! But their maps took different forms that Europeans didn't understand. Arab mapmakers knew what was there—and had drawn the maps to prove it. But Europeans were on their own fact-finding missions, and didn't take other people's findings into account.

On to America

Now once again the church played a role in mapping. Spain had gotten into the exploring act, sending Christopher Columbus west in the hope of finding an even faster route to the Indies than the Portuguese route that went around Africa. In 1494, the pope drew a line down the map from north to south. New land west of this Line of Demarcation would belong to Spain, and land to the east would be Portugal's. Apparently this agreement included ownership of all the resources in these lands, as well as the people.

In 1501, a Portuguese ship headed for Africa was blown off course across the Atlantic to South America, and its captain, Pedro Alvares Cabral, laid claim to Brazil. Amerigo Vespucci, an Italian traveler, mapped the coast of Brazil, adding more than 3,000 miles to the map of the coast of South America. He claimed to reach South America in 1497, a year before Columbus, which would have made him the first European to set foot on the continent. (Columbus' voyages took him to islands, not continents.) Some say Vespucci never even went to the Americas, though. Some say he went but lied about the year. Still, his claims were enough to get his name included on a map of the area. When Martin Waldseemüller created the first globe including the New World, he labeled the strip of land between the

A.D. 1200s–1600s European portolani—guides to coastal waters— changed the way people navigated. But even bigger changes were coming as people tried to sail around the world, which—so far—lay flat on maps.

A.D. **1600s**
Exploration made maps better and better in terms of position, direction, and detail.

Atlantic and the Pacific "America." So much controversy arose that Waldseemüller took the *America* label off future maps, but the name stuck anyway.

By 1513, explorers from Spain "discovered" the Pacific Ocean, explored Florida, and claimed Central America and southern North America. Vasco Nuñez de Balboa founded the first European colony on the American mainland, in Panama. On a hunt for riches and power, Hernan Cortés made his way to the capital of the Aztecs, Tenochtitlan, and conquered it. The land he claimed is now Mexico. His countryman, Francisco Pizarro, conquered Cuzco, the capital of the Incas, and founded Peru, before the natives killed him. Another Spaniard, Francisco Vasquez de Coronado, thought he'd found the Seven Cities of Cibola (a place he'd heard about in stories) when he found a pueblo in what is now the southwestern United States. The pueblo natives had plenty of silver—and soon Spain did, too.

By the early 1600s, the French arrived in Canada, and the Dutch and English planted flags in North America and Africa. Settlers arrived to hold down the ownership their countries claimed. Many of them came looking for religious freedom, but that didn't stop them from believing that their way was the right way—and that natives should get out of the way. At first, many lived side by side with

MAPMAKERS

Brooklyn Green Mappers

These mappers in Brooklyn, New York, mapped the new route garbage trucks would take when a big landfill shut down.

During two years, Brooklyn kids made Green Maps (see page 18) about two different aspects of the environment in their part of New York City. The Community Gardens Map showed more than just the vacant lots and parks that had been turned into gardens by neighbors; it showed a bike route that the kids planned, rode, and mapped from one garden to the next. Green Map users could tour Brooklyn by bike and stop at natural food stores, public parks, and tourist attractions along the way.

The next year, Green Mappers had a question they wanted answered. Now that the big landfill at Fresh Kills, Staten Island—the world's largest—would close down in 2001, where would the city's garbage go? To find out, mappers followed the garbage trucks, mapping their routes, and traced the routes that trucks would begin to follow once Fresh Kills closed.

They learned that some of the poorest areas of Brooklyn, Red Hook, and Greenpoint/Williamsburg, would be used as waste transfer stations. Greenpoint stations were already up and running. Red Hook was next. The city's garbage would be trucked there, and then loaded on barges and taken elsewhere.

Their map made the information easy to see: The city's poorest neighborhoods would have to put up with the smell and mess of everyone else's garbage.

For more about Green Maps, check out www.greenmap.org/nyc on the Web.

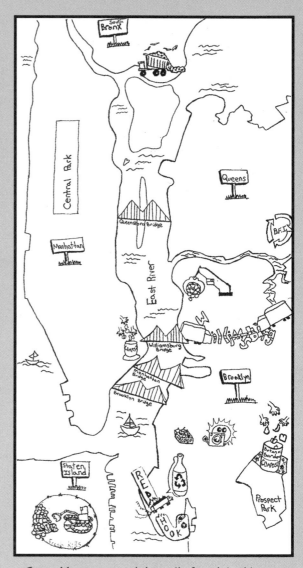

Green Mappers traced the trail of trash in this map.

the natives, but that only worked as long as maps didn't come into play. Once ownership of a place was established (and maps labeled with the owners' names), natives were forced to move out and move on. Sometimes settlers went to war with the natives and with other countries that tried to claim the same land.

The new settlers spread out from their coastal towns, exploding out of those known places into new land. And, of course, they added those new lands to their maps. In this way, Africa, Australia, parts of Asia, South America, and North America fell under the influence of European countries.

The Age of Taking Over?

Throughout the Age of Discovery—and the age of taking over that followed— new settlers fought battles over land rights and boundaries.

1744
This map of France—the first major national survey—was worked on by three generations of the Cassini family and took 11 years. It was published in 1744.

- Settlers in the United States fenced their land to show whose land was whose. Coyotes ignored the fences and stole sheep that were in territory they considered theirs. Today, Americans still disagree about whether ranchers should be allowed to fence federal (government) land. They disagree about what coyotes should be allowed to do, too.

- Native Americans who farmed the North American plains burned the land to prepare for planting, and sometimes they burned right through new homesteads. Boundaries and fences were also big trouble for native people who migrated, moving from place to place over the course of the year.

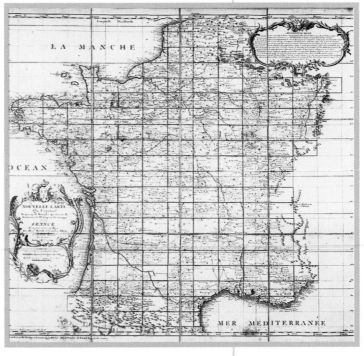

- Missionaries in African villages grew their own crops, only to find that they were expected to share. What grew in a village, villagers felt, was the shared property of all who lived there. It was against local customs and values for one person to keep his land or his crops to himself.

- Australian Aborigines live in what they call The Dreaming, an imagined universe that connects with the physical world through Songlines. The Songlines crisscross Australia. For Aborigines, the song is like a route. Their map is musical. What happened when European settlers began laying

MAPMAKER

Denis Wood

Cartographer Denis Wood has made many maps of his town, Boynton Hills, Illinois. Wood mapped the sewer system, including the drains, hydrants, and manhole covers. He mapped the trees, the traffic signs, and the pumpkins on porches at Halloween. He even mapped the houses of people whose names appeared in a local newspaper. And when he compared his maps, he found out some interesting—and weird—things. For example, he learned that the most traffic signs appeared on streets where people from out of the neighborhood were likely to drive. On back streets, where most of the drivers were people from the neighborhood, there were fewer signs. Another example: Wood found that the people whose names appeared in the paper most were the same ones who decorated their porches with pumpkins. His conclusion: Such people are reaching out to the community, wanting to be more involved than others.

fences? The Aborigines had to beg for their land. It was hard for them to understand physical boundaries. And it was hard for the Europeans to understand imaginary ones.

When a European drew a map of a new place, he didn't just draw its natural features. He drew boundaries and named places. And he drew them as he saw them and wanted them to be. All over the world, mapmakers set the course of history.

"Good fences make good neighbors," wrote American poet Robert Frost. But do they? There is more than one way to own land. Many people—and some countries—have built walls to make sure the boundaries aren't moved. Birds use their songs to mark out territory. Lions use urine. People use flags—and maps. Maps are one way to show who owns what. But check a recent map. Have national boundaries stayed the same?

Most of the wars fought in the world have had something to do with territory. Professional cartographers stay in business drawing world maps that show new boundaries, new countries, new divisions in old countries. Even in small towns, maps often change as land is sold or used in new ways. It was this way back when people never went farther than a few miles from home. Will it be this way when new universes are mapped? It's possible. If people can get to a place, they will want to know who owns it.

United Real Estate

The United States was built on maps. George Washington's first job—when he was a teenager—was as a surveyor. *Surveying* is a method of measuring land. The measurements are built into maps to show the distances, land features, and, yes, who owns what. Washington's surveying experience—and the understanding of the land that came with it—helped the colonies win the Revolutionary War. At important moments, Washington usually knew exactly where he was, and the British often didn't.

When the war ended, Washington became president, and his surveying knowledge was put to use expanding the new country beyond the original 13 colonies. Washington wasn't the first mapmaker to think that drawing a piece of land on a piece of paper was a good way of opening the discussion about whose land it was.

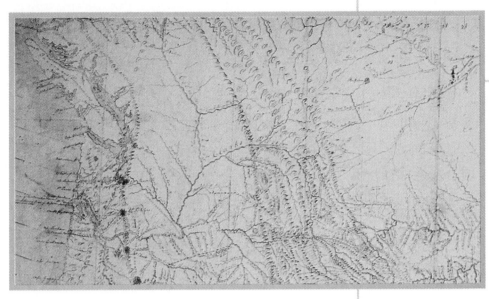

Look at a present-day map of the states, counties, and roads of the United States, and you can get an idea of how the West was won. West of the Appalachian Mountains, all the roads run in neat rectangles. This land was opened for settlement by Thomas Jefferson. Jefferson created the U.S. Public Land Survey System. Surveyors divided the land into those rectangular counties and townships. Even land that had no settlers had ownership and a new name. Today's maps of the United States show mainly four-sided shapes that reflect the way the land was surveyed.

Jefferson, like Washington, understood the power of a map. When he sent Meriwether Lewis and William Clark to explore west of the Mississippi to the Pacific Ocean, he had a map in mind. Early Americans—including Jefferson—thought it was America's destiny to be a country that stretched from sea to sea. Lewis and Clark were hunting for a river that would connect the Mississippi River to the Pacific. They were also noting information that would help them map the western territory.

Eventually, settlers needed to go to those areas if the United States was going to claim them. At the end of the 19th century, when a flood of European immigrants added to the population of the east coast, the government opened western states to homesteaders. If you could build a homestead and live on the land for five years, it was yours. Mapmakers carved the West into squares and rectangles, numbered them, and parceled them out. It was mainly up to settlers to "deal with" whatever—and whomever—they found when they reached their land.

Native Americans—like Sacagawea, Lewis and Clark's guide, or Doña

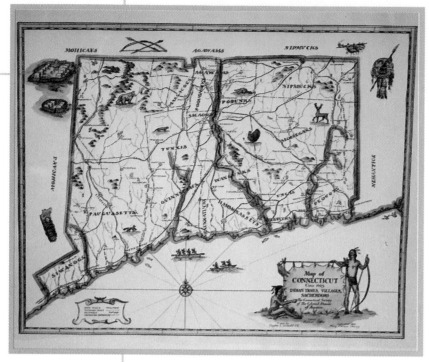

Compare these 16th-century Native American roads with . . .

. . . 1920s highways.

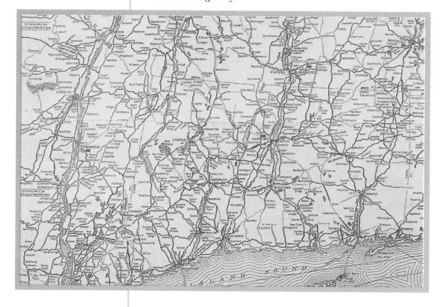

Marina, the Aztec woman who helped Cortés explore Mexico—knew their land well enough to lead explorers through it. Did they know what the explorers would do with the information they gathered? That data went back to mapmakers who added it to their base maps. And it became a huge factor as Europeans claimed land where native people had already made their homes. The more the newcomers knew, the more they mapped, and the more they claimed as their own.

There may be no better evidence of the civilizations that colonists overcame than the maps themselves. A 1920s map of Connecticut's just-paved road system looked a lot like a map of Native American roads in the 1600s. The Native Americans chose paths in the most convenient places running to the most desirable destinations. Settlers shared these first, then took them over, and the most used were paved over first. Some Native American trails had even deeper roots. Out West, they had been trampled by migrating bison. The tribes that hunted the bison followed these trails, which eventually formed the foundations of some of the roads that were paved across the West. In the East, roads started as deer trails.

In 1879, the United States began a national mapping program—the U.S. Geological Survey—which continues today. Its goal is to keep on mapping the United States, providing up-to-date maps for every inch of the country. The U.S. Geological Survey continues to add *quadrangle maps*, in which latitude and longitude

MY MAP AND ME

Nain Singh

The Himalayan mountains were first mapped in the 1860s by Nain Singh. Singh, a schoolmaster, was hired to add data to the Great Trigonometrical Survey, in which surveyors used triangulation to map India. Singh set out from India through Nepal to the mysterious land of Tibet, where outsiders were forbidden to enter. "A survey assignment in those days could be equivalent to a death sentence," wrote John Noble Wilford in his book *The Mapmakers,* where he told Singh's story.

Singh disguised himself as a poor lama, a monk on pilgrimage to the holy city of Lhasa. He had to hide his surveying equipment for fear that he would be caught, identified as a foreigner, and imprisoned or killed. From the window of his inn, he worked in secret to determine Lhasa's elevation. Although his movements were closely watched and he was often questioned, he managed to survey a 2000-km trade route from Nepal to Lhasa and to describe its position accurately on a map of Asia.

1866
Triangles were measured to map India accurately.

lines form a rectangle, or quadrangle. Put together all the quadrangles like a puzzle, and you have a detailed view of the United States. For the latest quadrangle map of your area, check out the Web site www.usgs.gov. You can see a sample on page 61.

Yes, the surface of the earth has mostly been explored. But people are still on the move, exploding out from the known world to the unknown world. In 1999, a scientist named Mike Fay began a 1,500-mile trek through the Congo Basin of Africa, traveling mostly in the country of Gabon. Along the way, he took notes on everything he encountered, from elephant dung to insects to tree species to monkeys that were friendly because they hadn't learned to fear humans—because they'd never seen any. Pygmy tribesmen who came along as jungle guides helped Fay with basic jungle survival, but they hadn't come this way before, either. A photographer who traveled with Fay for a little while figured that Fay's findings would feed fact-hungry scientists and mappers for years to come—just as Columbus' travels fed information to mappers of his time. There were no roads to follow, not even a footpath. The paths that Fay followed had never been trodden by people, only by elephants.

CHAPTER 3

The Whole World in Your Hands

The first map that showed the whole world—the Old World of Asia, Africa, and Europe, and the New World of North and South America—was published in 1493 by Juan de la Cosa, who had traveled with Columbus.

The worldview put together by the European explorers came about just at the time when scientists were drawing their most incredible conclusions about the way the earth fit into the universe. They realized that the earth was one of several planets that orbited the sun and, therefore, was not the center of the universe. This was the Age of Discovery—not just of new lands, but of new ideas about the world.

Mapmakers began to bring together the best information about every place that people were likely to travel. During the 1500s, cartographers from Italy and the Netherlands published the best world maps that had ever been drawn. In the late 1500s, a Dutch cartographer, Gerard Mercator, worked to create a new atlas, which was published after his death. Mercator is remembered because of his global view—and because he tried to build ideas about the round world into his flat map.

1992
The world's biggest globe, called Eartha, spins in Yarmouth, Maine. It is 42 feet in diameter.

Mapping the Seven Seas

A map is only as good as the mapmaker.

Ptolemy was considered the authority, and many mapmakers wouldn't give up using his map as a starting point. Christopher Columbus, sailing for China, never got past the Caribbean islands. What went wrong? Columbus didn't know how far away China was or how long it would take to get there. It's not true that Columbus didn't know the world was round. He did, thanks to Ptolemy. But

MY MAP AND ME

Dave Kunst

Dave Kunst left home (Waseca, Minnesota) one day and walked east. Four years and five weeks later, he walked into Waseca from the west. But even Dave Kunst saw only a small portion of the world.

Kunst figures it took him 20 million steps to make it around the world—a total of 14,452 miles, with an estimated 31 footsteps per hundred feet. He went through 21 pairs of shoes. He got help from four mules and a car. "There really is a road all the way around the world," Kunst says, describing how he and his brothers searched maps for roads that went west to east.

When Kunst reached an ocean, he dipped a foot in it, then crossed by plane or boat. On the other side, he put his foot in again, then kept traveling east. Kunst began with one walking buddy and ended with another. After his brother John was killed in Afghanistan, another brother, Pete, joined the trek. In Australia, Kunst walked alone until a schoolteacher who was driving cross-country offered to carry his gear in her car. She drove along slowly beside Kunst while he walked. They fell in love and got married.

"When I see a big globe or world map someplace," Dave Kunst says, "I smile and think to myself, 'I walked that world.'"

Ptolemy had underestimated the size of the Atlantic Ocean, and neither he nor Columbus had any idea that the Pacific existed.

A ship entering new and risky waters often takes on a pilot, someone who knows the area. This is as true today as it was in Columbus' time. The first sailing directions for unfamiliar shores were passed from pilot to pilot. Eventually descriptions were written down. And later the directions became painted charts called *portolani*. As people explored more, sailed farther, and got better at navigation, the charts improved. Eventually they were used as the basis of national coastal surveys. But the portolani focused on coasts. What happened when people turned their backs on the shore and headed for the open oceans?

In 1519, Ferdinand Magellan set off west from Portugal toward South America and around the world. He carried no map, and he didn't know how big the Pacific was or how long it would take to cross it. After all, he was going somewhere that hadn't been mapped.

It was 1522 before Magellan's ship arrived home, without Magellan on it. An Italian nobleman, Antonio Pigafetta, who went along as an unpaid crew member, kept a journal of notes and drawings. Magellan had died in the Philippines, but Pigafetta and his journal made it home. It was because of him that, for the first time, a map of the world was based on someone's firsthand experience of it.

Putting the Pieces Together

The only way human beings can get an idea of the world is by relying on other people's views of it—*many* other people's.

Abraham Ortelius' *Theatrum Orbis Terrarum* ("Theater of the World"), published in 1570, was a dramatic and beautiful atlas. But, like most mapmakers of his time, Ortelius copycatted Ptolemy. If there wasn't any new information about a place, he let the old information stand. Even though maps by the likes of Mercator and Waldseemüller were available by 1600, plenty of travelers—including some of the most famous European explorers—kept right on following Ptolemy's ideas. Long past 1600, maps still existed that used Ptolemy's map measurements and land and sea descriptions.

Two hundred years after Magellan's voyage, the Pacific Ocean was still unexplored and unmapped. A few small islands appeared on new maps, but the Pacific was still a blank until Abel Tasman arrived from the Netherlands. Tasmania—and the marsupial called the Tasmanian devil—was named after him. Tasman mapped New Zealand and part of the west and north coasts of Australia.

For centuries, mapmakers had sketched in *Terra Australis Incognita*, the "Unknown Southern Land," even though they didn't know it existed. When Australia was "discovered," the mapmakers thought they'd found the elusive southern continent. Europeans had no proof that a southern continent existed;

1522
If it weren't for a writer and artist named Antonio Pigafetta, little record would exist of Magellan's trip around the world. This map shows part of the Philippines.

TYPVS ORBIS TERRARVM

QVID EI POTEST VIDERI MAGNVM IN REBVS HVMANIS, CVI AETERNITAS
OMNIS, TOTIVSQVE MVNDI NOTA SIT MAGNITVDO. CICERO:

1570
When Dutch cartographer Abraham Ortelius published his Theatrum Orbis Terrarum, "Theater of the World," he used the information that was available to him at the time.

they simply thought that one was needed in order to balance out the landmasses in the Northern Hemisphere. Antarctica wouldn't be spotted until 1820, and its existence wasn't proved until the end of the 19th century.

Australia and Antarctica weren't all that was missing from the maps. Until the three voyages of Captain Cook, beginning in 1768, hundreds of islands across the Pacific were off the map. A map of Captain Cook's travels looks like he played connect-the-dots with every point along the coast and many of the islands. Because he sailed from England, his journeys included many Atlantic stops, too. His last trip, begun in 1776, included Brazil, the Cape of Good Hope, Tasmania, New Zealand, Tonga, Tahiti, Hawaii, Alaska, and back to Hawaii, which he named the Sandwich Islands. And there the journey ended, as Hawaiians—who first thought Cook was a god arriving in answer to their call—put him to death.

Visitors to Hawaii were amazed to find that the people there, the Polynesians, shared appearance, stories, and customs with people living on other Pacific islands thousands of miles away. The Polynesians knew that their ancestors had traveled all that way by boat. They weren't just blown off course, either. They had a plan

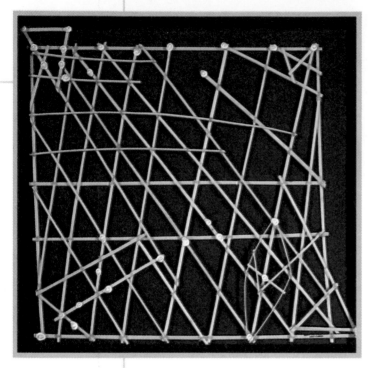

by 1000
The shells in this woven map from the Marshall Islands stood for islands in the South Pacific. The palm fibers showed the direction and pattern of ocean waves.

and maps—in the form of woven grasses and shells, as well as instructions about how to navigate that were passed down by word of mouth—to help them find their way across the Pacific. But again, it was Europeans who brought together information and made it into world maps.

Captain Cook learned his trade far from the South Pacific, in Newfoundland, Canada, where he charted 1,800 miles of coast. He became expert at math and at using the stars to find his way. When the British Navy first sent him to the South Pacific, part of his job was to watch the movements of Venus. Astronomers hoped that seeing the stars from the Southern Hemisphere would help them find the distances between the Sun, the Moon, Earth, and the other planets. They were wrong, and the measurements wouldn't be accurately made for many years. But Cook's Pacific voyages helped solve a different kind of measurement problem: how to find longitude.

The Longitude Problem

People had learned to measure the land well by the 1700s. They could pinpoint their own positions pretty well, and they could figure out the distances between places accurately. If cartographers were going to get their maps right, all over the world, they were going to have to do a good job measuring the oceans, as well as the land. A key to this was solving the longitude problem at sea.

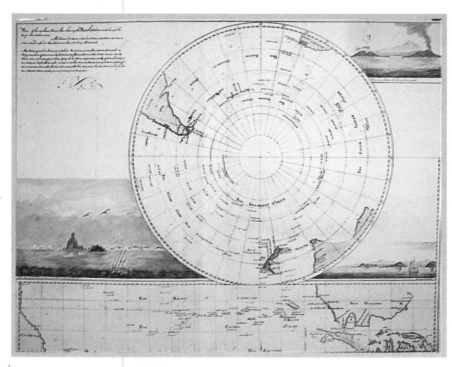

1775
Captain Cook mapped the Pacific but never spotted Antarctica. This map is based on what he did and didn't find.

MY MAP AND ME

Dan Dillon

Dan Dillon's company, Replogle Globe, has made a lot of globes—70 million of them, in fact. If you laid them side by side, they'd go pretty far. And you could go pretty far with the information on them, too.

Dillon declares, "A globe certainly is better than a flat map!" Then he settles down. "I'm not trying to take a shot at maps," he explains. "But a globe shows a true perspective view of the world, in its true proportions."

If you want to understand how the world works, Dillon says, a globe is your best tool. "You can use a flashlight to shine like the sun on your globe, and figure out how the sun can come up on the East Coast of the United States while it's still dark on the West Coast. You can spin the globe to understand the rotation of the earth. In the winter, the sun is shining on the Southern Hemisphere, in the summer it's shining on the Northern Hemisphere."

Why does the world buy so many globes a year—from Replogle and other globe manufacturers? "People want to understand the world," Dillon says. "They feel more worldly if they have a globe. And, it's a nice, decorative item."

Globes are constantly updated to reflect changes in the borders of nations and new knowledge about the world. The gores are glued onto a spherical base—a ball—so that they make one continuous image. Here, gores are designed so that they fit together precisely.

When these globes have dried, they'll be set on bases at a tilt. Why? It's easy to imagine that the north–south axis of the earth stays vertical as Earth orbits the sun. But Earth tilts. In late December, the top half of Earth tilts away from the sun. The bottom half tilts toward the sun. With a globe, you can get around without ever leaving home.

It was simple enough to measure latitude by checking the angle of the sun. But the sun and stars were no help in finding longitude. Because sailors couldn't measure longitude, they couldn't figure out their global position. As a result, ships wrecked all over the world. The navigators made mistakes about where they were and what dangers they were near. Solving the problem was a huge issue, and huge prizes were offered by the British government to anyone who could solve it. John Harrison won the prize by creating a clock that could keep time anywhere, under any circumstances.

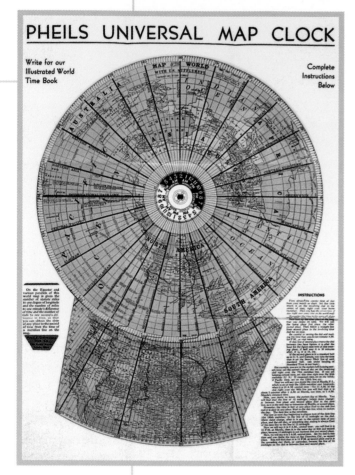

PHEILS UNIVERSAL MAP CLOCK

A dial, rotating around the center point, shows time around the world. There are 24 longitude lines and 24 time zones. They don't match because time zones are set up for practical reasons, not only geographic ones.

The key to measuring longitude was time. The round earth is divided up into 24 time zones, one for each hour of the day, and each measuring 15 degrees at the equator. If a ship captain knew what time it was in his home port *and* what time it was where he was located, then he could do the math to find out what his longitude was. Harrison's *marine chronometer* did what no clock had ever been able to do—keep time correctly on ship. The solution of the longitude problem added precision to mapping at sea. Captain Cook carried one of the brand-new marine chronometers on his second journey, begun in 1772. The chronometer allowed him to pinpoint his position every time he spotted something new he wanted to map.

Maps of the world could now be precise about global position, giving the exact location of any place, whether they covered land or sea. For the first time, the globe could be measured accurately—and global position could be figured out precisely.

Let Me Tell You About My Planet

In ancient times, while many people were thinking about owning parts of the earth, a few were looking up at the stars and wondering what—and where—the earth was. Here are some of the stories people used to tell about the way the earth worked:

- Earth was a flat disk supported by four elephants standing on a turtle's back.
- Earth was a flat disk floating on water.
- Earth was square.
- Earth was held up on pillars by Atlas.
- Earth was a flat disk resting on top of a cylinder.

It was the dome of the sky that first helped people to understand that Earth was a sphere.

The earliest globes didn't show the earth, they showed the sky. These *celestial globes* were made of stone or copper by astronomers in Mesopotamia, Egypt, and Greece, around 500 B.C. Terrestrial globes came later. First, people had to figure out that Earth was round, too.

MAPS MAKE THE DIFFERENCE
Internet Eratosthenes

Karen Nishimoto's seventh grade class at Punahou School in Honolulu, Hawaii, set out to imitate the globe-measuring experiment Eratosthenes did in Greece 2,200 years ago. Although Eratosthenes had to travel from Alexandria to Cyrene, the Urchins—the team that did this project—sent e-mails to other schools, from Seattle to Maine. Their aim was to figure out the distance from their school to the others, and to calculate what percentage of 360 degrees that distance represented. When they got stuck, they even e-mailed Nobel scientist Arno Penzias for advice. He advised them to use a globe instead of a flat map.

The Urchins got to work. Alex made a globe out of modeling clay, and Kawika set up an overhead projector to take the place of the sun. Elise plotted their findings on graph paper, and Melanie studied them to see how the data related to one another. "Triumphant screams broke out as the numbers came in," Nishimoto says.

Do it yourself at http://youth.net/eratosthenes/welcome.html

Aryabhata, an astronomer living in India in 500 B.C., said that the stars circled Earth in the night sky because Earth spun like a top.

Some Chinese astronomers around 150 B.C. thought Earth was a hemisphere under a dome-shaped universe. Others quoted an old Chinese saying: "Heaven is like an egg, and the earth is like the yolk of the egg." Still others thought the universe was huge empty space where celestial bodies floated around—close to the truth!

Getting a complete picture of our world has taken a long time. The idea that we're on a big spinning ball zooming through space at thousands of miles per hour isn't a quick conclusion to reach. Watch closely next time you're at the beach and spot a boat heading out to sea. The bottom of the boat seems to slip below the horizon. The mast goes next. And the little flag on top goes last of all.

People watching for ships long ago noticed this, too. They also observed that they could see their ships come in a few minutes earlier if they watched from cliffs or rooftops. Being on higher ground let them see above the curvature of the earth. People with their eyes on the horizon began to wonder if the world was round.

Widow's walks on shore houses let people get an early glimpse of the flags of returning ships— proof that the world is round.

In the Shadow of the Sun

In about 250 B.C., a Greek mathematician named Eratosthenes heard about a post that cast no shadow at noon on the day of the summer solstice. It was in Cyrene,

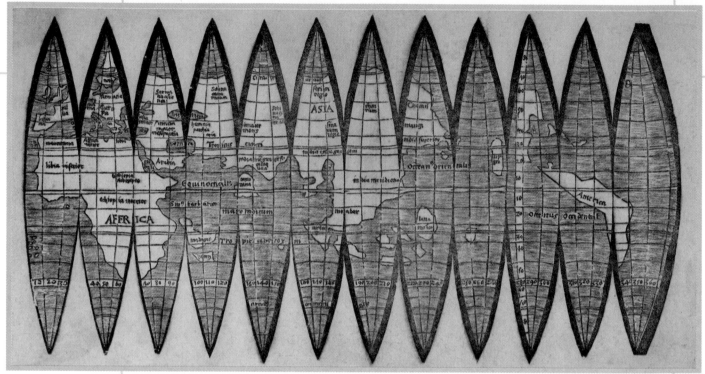

1507

Martin Waldseemüller of Germany published a world map and globe that became very popular with new explorers and with armchair travelers— people who liked to imagine exploring. Can you imagine how these gores fit over a sphere to make a globe?

a town south of Alexandria in Egypt. But in Alexandria, posts cast shadows. Eratosthenes figured that the Sun must be shining its light on the two towns at two different angles. Therefore, he thought, the earth must be curved. Eratosthenes found the distance between the two cities and calculated the angle of the post to the shadow. He determined the girth of the earth to be 7,850 miles (12,633 kilometers). He was only 76 miles off! Up until then, nobody had ever proved Earth was round, never mind measured it.

Another Greek, Hipparchus, helped lay the foundations of scientific cartography—maps based on numbers, not stories—that used a globe as the form of Earth. He also drew the first lines of latitude and longitude. But nobody paid much attention to Erastosthenes and Hipparchus.

In about 200 B.C., a Greek man named Aristarchus said Earth revolved around the sun. Crates of Mallus, a Greek, made what may have been the first *terrestrial globe*—one that showed Earth. That was about 140 B.C. Like Ptolemy, Crates didn't know how big Earth was.

Some early flat maps showed the world as a disk surrounded by ocean waters. The ocean formed a letter O around the land. The land was divided into three continents by important bodies of water in the shape of a T. The continents were Europe, Asia, and Africa. The bodies of water were the Nile, the Mediterranean, and the Don. The *T-O* map showed real geographical features, but it wasn't true in terms of directions and distances. Some mappers even thought the flat disk sat on top of a column.

All through the Middle Ages, some explorations were made, but little was added to people's understanding of the way the world worked. Maps didn't improve much, either. In A.D. 1200–1300, Arab astronomers used sun shadows to measure Earth's size, as Eratosthenes did. This information, too, made no dent on people's thinking.

Martin Behaim's 1492 globe—which he called an Earth Apple—came closer to the right proportions—but still didn't have the measurements right. Martin Waldseemüller's globe, made of gores created in the same year as his flat map of the world, was the first to show the New World. You can trace Waldseemüller's gores onto a sheet of paper. Cut out the gores and shape them over a tennis ball. Use straight pins to hold them together at the poles. What happens when you do the reverse and try to shape an orb into a flat piece of paper? It's about as simple as flattening out your tennis ball. Grab an orange, instead.

Flattening out the Globe

Write your name all the way around the outside of an orange. Write in big, fat letters. Cover the whole skin. Now try to peel your orange so that your name looks right. You'll have to make top and bottom slits to make the peel lie flat.

You're facing some of the same problems cartographers have as they try to make flat maps of a round world. It can't be done perfectly. Globes are the only representation of Earth that show lands and oceans in terms of size and position. Only globes can show a place with correct distances, areas, and angles. It's impossible on a two-dimensional map.

To make any flat map, something is always given up—distances, areas, or angles get lost or distorted, stretched, or shrunken. So why do people bother with flat maps?

It's a big world, after all. Globes can only show Earth at a very small scale. A globe that is 12 inches in diameter is 41.8 million times smaller than Earth. To get a detailed view of any area, you'd need to have a very large globe.

Can a globe be made into a flat map?

Flat maps are the only way to get the detail necessary to understand what a place is like. So, mapmakers—and travelers—have figured out *projections*—mathematical formulas that let them use flat maps to show the information they need and get where they want to go.

MAP MAKER

Peter W. Sloss

Peter Sloss is up to his neck in globes and maps. At least that's how he made it look when he used his computer to make this picture of his office at the National Geophysical Data Center in Boulder, Colorado. But it's not the only special effect he knows how to do. Sloss uses a computer to convert numbers (such as elevation) into shapes and colors on maps. Sloss's globe views are *orthographic projections*. They are flat—but they show how the world would look from different perspectives, if you could fly away from Earth and then look back.

Not being able to see around the curve—as you can with a flat map—is what makes an orthographic projection undistorted.

"It's more realistic because it's correct in scale and position. No, you can't see it all at once, but you can if you look at all the different views." To see those views, check out the National Geophysical Data Center's site at www. noaa.ngdc.gov.

Peter W. Sloss of the National Geophysical Data Center, is up to his neck (almost) in maps and globes.

Projections–Quite a Project

Mercator's projection, in his atlas published in 1599, let him draw the round world in a flat way, showing the correct angles between things, if not the correct distances.

One easy way to identify a Mercator projection is by comparing landmasses close to the poles with landmasses on a globe. Greenland is the classic example. On a Mercator projection, Greenland is eight times larger than its real size, which is a big error. But, Mercator users figure most people aren't going to Greenland. And on a Mercator projection, countries closer to the equator—where more people live—are drawn more accurately.

On the floor of a tower in a French observatory, the Cassini family drew a circular map with the North Pole at the center. (The Cassinis were into triangles, as well as circles. See page 39.) As the Global Position of places was determined and carefully fixed, they were added to the map. Explorers were sent all over the world to measure, plot, and send back data. In 1696, the tower map was transferred to paper at last. This map became the standard for world maps published in the early 18th century. The Cassini Planisphere showed the positions and shapes of landmasses as accurately as the Cassinis could. But the specifics were mostly wrong.

The problem for mapmakers and the people who use their maps is to draw maps that show positions of places in such a way that people can navigate from one to the next without going off course—a challenge with a flat map.

Cartographers are still working to come up with different ways to make a flat map out of a round world. Yes, they have to give up distances or angles or areas. They can show how far apart two things are, or they can show what angle they are from each other—but not both.

Albers Equal Area
and
Lambert Conformal Conic
Projections
Origin 39 N, 96 W
Standard Parallels 33 N and 45 N

Albers Equal Area

Lambert Conformal Conic

But in most cases, it's possible to make a map that shows what you need most.

Projections are different methods for transferring the round surface of the earth to a flat surface, making a sphere into a plane. The goal is to reproduce the earth or a portion of the earth with a minimum of distortion. The cartographer must select the projection best suited to the use of the map.

On globes, latitude lines are parallel and are spaced equally on the longitude lines (meridians). The meridians meet at the poles. They are farthest apart (15 degrees) at the equator, the same distance apart as the parallels. As you look at different map projections, notice how the longitude and latitude lines are distorted. Which lines you decide to distort depends on how your map will be used—and it determines which projection your map will have. Here are a few of the most popular map projections:

- **Mercator** Longitude lines are usually parallel at the equator, but they come together and meet at the poles. A Mercator projection makes all the longitude lines parallel, so any course you set using this map is a straight line. Cartographers who use the Mercator projection figure that most map users will be traveling in the more temperate zones, not in the frozen north or south, where most of the distortions are on a Mercator map.

- **Conformal** If you really want to see how big Greenland is, check a conformal projection. The scale is true—but the angles (directions) between places aren't.

- **Equal-area** To get a better idea of place sizes and angles, try an equal-area projection. The problem here? The *shape* of places is distorted.

How do two projections of the same place compare? The red lines are the Albers Equal Area projection. The green lines are the Lambert Conformal Conic Projection. Compare the same area on a globe. What's different?

The Politics of Projections

Differences between projections may be shocking or subtle. And people have often been known to use them to suit their own needs in ways other than to measure or navigate. Say, for example, you want to make your country seem strong and powerful. It's possible to choose a projection that gives your country a new look.

Mark Monmonier is a professor of geography at Syracuse University in New York. On his U.S. map on page 57, Rhode Island is a lot bigger than usual. "Some people don't like my map because it distorts boundaries, rivers, and things," Monmonier says. "The point wasn't to show those things." The point of the map was to help people compare information—such as number of voters or number of dogs—in the states. "A map shows lots of different kinds of information. You have to design it in a way that helps people see the information you're showing. You must choose what you want to emphasize."

New Paths Around the World

Thanks to the marine chronometer, figuring out where you were—based on longitude and time—had never been easier than it was by the 1800s. But it was still a *marine* chronometer, which was most helpful to mariners—people on ships, that is. What about land? Now that people all over the world were making maps, mapmakers wanted a worldwide system of measurement.

The International Convention of the Meter took place in 1875. The meter stood for one 10-millionth of the distance from the North Pole to the equator. The idea of the meter came from a Frenchman named Gabriel Mouton in the late 1700s. By the time the meter was officially approved in 1875, it was no longer a true 10-millionth. If it were, the standard quadrant (fourth) of the meridian would be exactly 10 million meters. Instead, it's 10,002,001.23 meters. Mistakes were still being made about the exact size of the globe.

Here we are in the third millennium. Don't we have accurate maps of the world yet? Far from it. In 1891, the International Map of the World project was begun. A group of cartographers from all over the world established standards of scale and symbols and began to put together a detailed map, all measured in meters, the new standard of measurement. A Central Bureau of the Map of the World was set up in England. The cartographers would go off to do their jobs and send the results to Central.

But the world map project was slow going. Although nearly 40 countries were producing maps, only eight of the 2,500 maps needed had been finished by 1914.

MAPS MAKE THE DIFFERENCE

Mark Monmonier

Mark Monmonier is a professor of geography at Syracuse University in New York and an authority on how maps can be used to change how people see places. His book *How to Lie with Maps* shows how people use maps to emphasize what they want emphasized. Some are pretty innocent—like a store that creates a map showing customers how to get there, leaving out other stores. Others have a plan in mind, such as the redrawing of maps of voting districts so that more voters from one party are in the district than another—helping one candidate to get elected.

Monmonier told me this story about a fight between mapmakers. "A historian named Arno Peters showed a world map called 'Peters' Map of the World.'" This projection—an equal-area projection—has lots of distortion in the tropics near the equator where many Third World countries are.* Peters claimed cartographers—who usually didn't use this projection—were unfair to Third World countries by making them look too small and unimportant.

"Even bad maps can work really well." Peters was right that Third World countries needed help, Monmonier says, but wrong about his mapmaking. "If you want to be fair to Third World countries, use a demographic map [one that shows the number of people in countries] rather than focusing on their area."

* Third World countries are places where development has been slower than in other parts of the world. They are usually poorer.

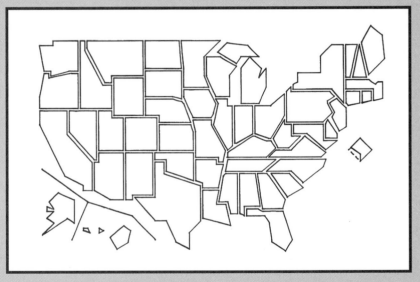

Different purposes . . . different projections. Mark Monmonier created this U.S. map to help show each state clearly—even the tiniest states.

By the 1930s, more than 400 maps had turned up at Central, but many didn't follow the rules that had been set up so that the maps would match. In the 1940s, during World War II, the Central Bureau offices—and the maps inside—were destroyed by bombs. The United Nations took over after the war, but many nations had lost interest. By the 1980s, the project had faded away. The effort to put together lots of little pictures hadn't worked. It would take a look at the big picture—the entire globe—before Earthlings would begin to truly understand the world.

CHAPTER 4

A Bird's-eye View

And then, something truly amazing happened. People got up above the earth and looked down.

In the 1700s, hot-air balloons helped humans rise above the earth for the first time. Our point of view changed, and so did our maps. The higher people went, the more we could see. We will never get tired of looking. And we will never stop finding new discoveries about the earth and new ways to view it.

How could we really understand the world before then? Way back around 450 B.C., the philosopher Socrates said that if we could rise above the earth we would realize the "true earth." People have long drawn maps as though from above, using their imaginations, but for thousands of years the highest they could go was a treetop or tall building.

In 19th-century America, mapmakers traveled from town to town looking for work. Once a town hired them, they spent much of their time on the highest hilltops, look-

What happens to mappers' perceptions of the world when they get off the ground?

ing down like hawks at the town below. The base of the map was a grid that showed the town's plan, its streets and open land. The mapmakers walked the streets taking notes and sketching, then filled in the grids with their findings. The maps these bird's-eye mapmakers drew were as much pictures as maps. They were maps that showed *topography*, physical features like hills, cliffs, woods, and ponds, as well as houses, roads, and railroad tracks. In a way, their work set the stage for the first aerial photographers, who took pictures from balloons or airplanes and turned them into maps.

The bird's-eye mapmakers drew from below the horizon, and the horizon appeared on their maps. Houses had sides, trees and hills were rounded. Church steeples towered over everything but mountains. And every feature had a shadow that showed its shape, as in the detailed relief maps that would come later. Such large-scale maps thrilled people because they allowed them to see great detail. For the first time, they had a chance to see their town at a glance—something you couldn't do unless you had wings.

While people were still earthbound, the only way to find out the information they needed was to go to a place and explore it. To get an idea of how difficult this could be, consider the Grand Canyon. If you travel

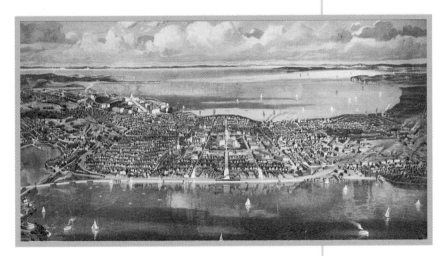

Bird's-eye views like this one of Madison, Wisconsin, were created by traveling mapmakers in the late 1800s.

Artist James Whistler showed what Anacapa Island, California, would look like from sea and air.

MY MAP AND ME

John Baird

John Baird, president of Unique Media Maps of Toronto, Canada, tells the story of a traveling bird's-eye-view mapmaker who was arrested in Pennsylvania during World War I. "He was thrown in jail because they thought he was doing some kind of spy work for the Germans. Why else would anyone want that kind of information?"

Unique Media publishes maps that show bird's-eye views for the 21st century—like this world map, something no bird has ever seen. For one thing, the oceans have shrunk. "The world is a mind's-eye kind of thing," Baird says. "What you put on it depends on your purpose. It's a practical matter, a matter of what people need to see to get information. In these days of air travel, the ocean's size doesn't signify much anyway. What's real when it comes to mapping?"

Wait a minute. Aren't maps supposed to be accurate? "The business of exaggerating features is done on every map, whether people realize it or not. Take a constant-scale road map. A major highway has to be shown out of scale with the rest of the map, or else you wouldn't be able to see the road."

As with other hand-drawn maps, Unique Media's take massive time and research. "Our map of the world took 5,000 hours," says Baird. "Art took up 4,000 hours. Research took up the rest. We gather photos from all over the world and use everything from satellite shots to ground-level shots as reference.

"People love maps more than ever before, I think," says Baird. "Since satellites and the space shuttle went up, since people landed on the Moon, there's been a huge increase in interest in what Earth looks like from above and from space."

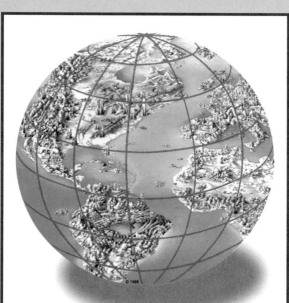

This map is a modern bird's-eye view. What kind of information can you get from it?

there today, you can still find medallions—brass circles that shine in the sun. Late 19th-century surveyors focused their instruments, called *theodolites*, on these medallions to measure the Grand Canyon in triangles. There are still many parts of the canyon where no person has ever set foot, unreachable crevices and valleys, peaks and pinnacles too hard to climb. The only way to measure and map them is to do it from afar. It was risky just to get to a place in the canyon where you could see one of these unreachable points, focus the theodolite, and then measure the horizontal and vertical angles of the medallion relative to its own position. That would allow him to use geometry to figure out the exact position of the medallion.

Today, satellites taking readings from space can survey the entire Grand Canyon in seconds.

A Sigh of Relief

Say you flew above the Grand Canyon at noon, when the shadows are shortest. The canyon from above would look far flatter than it would if you stood on its floor. Sure, you could outline its shape perfectly, and could draw a sort of floor map. But a floor map only shows the "footprint" of a feature—its outline as you look at it from above. A relief map shows the different heights and depths of land or water.

A shaded relief map, like this one of Mono Lake, has a shadow layer that shows features such as mountains, valleys, and bodies of water. It is designed to look like the sun is shining from one direction and casting shadows, so that different shapes can be seen. Without shadows, the land would look completely flat. Shaded relief maps do a good job of showing the different levels on a small scale. But if you really want to climb every mountain and get down into every valley, you need a large-scale map with contour lines.

Shadows on a shaded relief map show the shape, elevation, and depth of features.

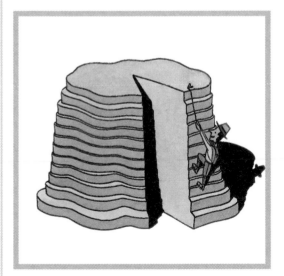

Imagine Mt. Pancake, a mountain cut into slices like pancakes. That's what contour mappers do when they map places with different elevations. Each pancake stands for a certain number of feet.

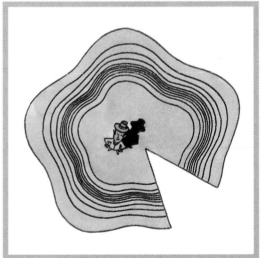

Here's a contour map of Mt. Pancake. Contour maps help you see how high or low a place is—even on a flat map.

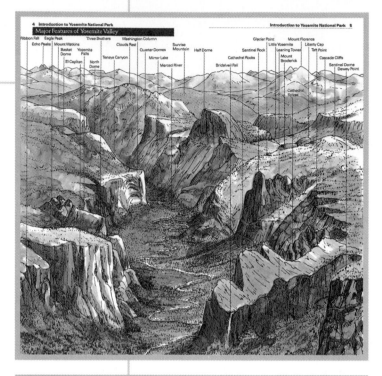

Compare the bird's-eye view of Yosemite Valley with the contour map of the same place.

Imagine slicing a mountain horizontally into slabs like pancakes. Say each pancake is 10 feet high and extends the whole width of the mountain. As you slice higher and higher, the pancakes get smaller and smaller, until the very top peak is just a little mound, like butter above your pancake stack. Now imagine that you looked down from a bird's-eye view above your pancake mountain. Draw the bottom pancake, then the next and the next and the next. Each one of those lines stands for one pancake—one 10-foot slab. What you're drawing are contour lines.

Contour lines show different land levels—elevations—from lowlands to mountains and craters, and water levels from underwater canyons to shallow lakes. Some maps with contour lines have colors that correspond to the elevations or depths, so that different colors indicate different levels. But contour maps can also be black and white. Either way, the closer the lines are together, the higher the mountains or deeper the canyons.

Up in the Air

Mapmakers knew that getting above the horizon would help them draw clearer maps. Getting there was the first problem. Staying there long enough to draw a map was the second problem. The answer lay in a quick click: a camera. Still, it wasn't an easy answer.

The first aerial photograph was taken by a French balloonist in 1858. But a photograph, although it can show plenty, isn't the same as a map. Why not?

Picture the earth from the side. It's curved. A balloonist flies up and takes a picture, pointing the camera lens straight down. Things in the center of the

MAPS MAKE THE DIFFERENCE

Trail-O Orienteering

Jordy Thompson, 13, spent last summer getting lost in the woods—and finding himself again, thanks to an orienteering map that helped the woods around him shape themselves into a race track with a starting point, stations called control points, and a finish line.

In orienteering, racers use a map with contour lines and symbols that show landmarks. "You find your way with a compass and the map," says Jordy, then adds, "hopefully." Along the way, orienteers have to find stations. Each control point has a marker—usually a special hole punch—so orienteers can prove they really made it to the control point. The winner is the one who finishes the route in the shortest time.

Jordy and his team of two walkers and two other kids in wheelchairs got lost the first time out. "We got our directions wrong because we read the compass wrong. We were supposed to go west, but we went north. When we realized we'd gone the wrong way, we went back to the beginning and figured it out again."

Since that first outing, Jordy has orienteered several times. "It seems like every time we'd go, there were more kids that knew what they were doing. Having the map helps me drive through the woods in my head first—and then I can just look at the map again if I get lost."

Jordy and his team took part in traditional orienteering, but they may soon have the chance to take part in Trail-O, a form with larger-scale orienteering maps (1:10,000 scale instead of 1:15,000) to reflect shorter distances between control points. This will let the maps be more exact, but, as Jordy says, getting stuck—and finding yourself again—is part of orienteering.

picture will be pretty much correct. But features on the edges of the picture will be distorted.

A Frenchman named Aimé Laussedat worked on this problem for some time. Long before 1858, he tried to attach a camera to a kite. No such luck! It was a balloon that carried up his next invention, the first camera made for mapping. It was a combination camera and theodolite. This was the beginning of *photogrammetry*, the science of measuring things accurately through photographs.

Photogrammetry really took off when airplanes did. In World War I, photos helped the military map enemy lands. As time went on, mapmakers got better at cutting down on distortion and making up for the tilt of plane or camera. And planes went higher and higher above the horizon. *Stereoscopes*—cameras that took two pictures of one thing so that, when viewed together, it looked three-dimensional—helped make aerial photograms accurate.

One flying cameraman, Sherman M. Fairchild, started developing mapping cameras in the 1920s, when planes stayed low to the ground. He was still inventing improvements in the 1960s, when *Apollo* astronauts used his cameras to map the moon. In between, the U.S. Geological Survey was one of many groups around the world to use aerial photogrammetry to map land. The man who began the U.S. aerial mapping program was named, of all things, Claude H. Birdseye.

The best view of any area is not just one bird's-eye view, but many. The best aerial photographs of the mid-20th century were mosaics, put together from pieces of many different photographs.

In the early 20th century, aerial photographers produced stereoscopes, which showed two views. If you've ever used a Viewmaster, you'll have an idea of the 3-D effect this produced. Compare this view of Egypt with the pyramid view on page 73 created a century later.

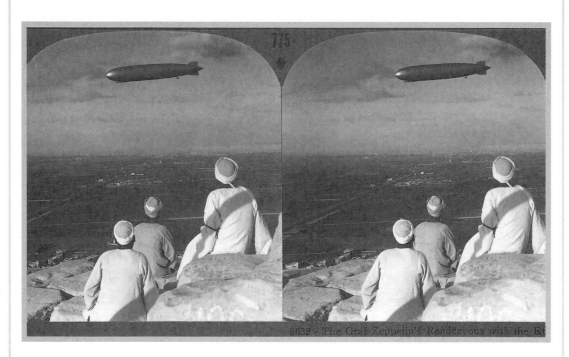

The U.S. Geological Survey matches quadrangle maps with aerial photographs to make orthophotoquadrangles, like this one of Miami, Florida.

MY MAP AND ME

Pete DeLeo

One moment Pete DeLeo was piloting his plane on a routine trip across California's Sierra Nevada Mountains. The next moment his plane was caught in turbulence and crashed in the mountains. DeLeo was suddenly on the ground with cracked ribs, no map, and winter closing in.

DeLeo knew where he was in the sky before the crash—but suddenly being on the ground made him see things in a different light. "You use a chart when you fly," DeLeo says. "It's called a 'sectional,' because it's a map of the section you're flying through." The sectional includes data for the plane's instruments, elevations of the land below, and information about traffic in the air-space the plane will pass through.

Because of his sectional map, DeLeo had a picture in his mind of the land below his plane. It was a short flight, and it had seemed like a small area to cross. When he found himself down on that land, it suddenly seemed very big. "What takes 45 minutes in the air could take you eight days on foot. It could be impassable. There could be a glacier in the way for all you know. Up in the air, there's an easy way out: a flick of the yoke (the plane's steering wheel) and we're on our way."

Instead, DeLeo had to walk out, find his way back to civilization. For the next two wintry weeks, he had to climb cliffs and sleep in caves. When a blizzard hit, he spent days inside a tree trunk. He struggled with hunger, broken bones from the crash, and frostbite.

"Usually the best thing to do is follow a stream," DeLeo advises. "The stream will lead to a bigger stream, and that will lead to a river, and pretty soon there will be a bridge. You'll climb up on the bridge and walk up the road for help." But DeLeo didn't know exactly where the rivers he found would lead. He did know that to the east lay Route 395, a highway. He watched the mountains to see which way lay east. "The snow melts fastest on the south side," DeLeo says. By figuring out south, he figured out east, and continued that way. The plane went down on November 27; DeLeo made it to the highway—and help—on December 9.

Out of This World

To do photogrammetry accurately from the air, you need to know how high off the ground your plane is. The U.S. Geological Survey planes, trying to get the same kind of information for every piece of land in the country, had to fly at the same altitude: 3,600 meters. If the planes' altitudes were constant, mapmakers could do the math they needed to make the maps match up with the land below.

As the space program began in the 1950s, rockets took cameras into orbit—and they took photogrammetry to new heights. Rockets traveling outside Earth's atmosphere were *remote*—far away. Besides cameras, they carried new instruments that *sensed* things about the earth. *Remote sensing technology* uses sensors in space to find information, signals from space to communicate, and computers on the ground to discover new things about the earth every single day. Some jobs were preprogrammed. Others were done by—you guessed it—remote control.

Remote sensing instruments don't just gather the kind of information a person gathers with five senses. They can measure gravity, magnetism, light and radio waves, and much more. The sensors collect data that computers use to make new maps. Throughout the first half of the 20th century, scientists developed remote sensing technology. But their instruments and machines and techniques needed a platform, some vehicle they could ride in order to look down at Earth.

The first photographs of Earth from space were shots of New Mexico that were taken by German V-2 rockets just after World War II. These spy shots were found by U.S. Army scientists when the rockets were captured. After this, the next space shots were taken from satellites.

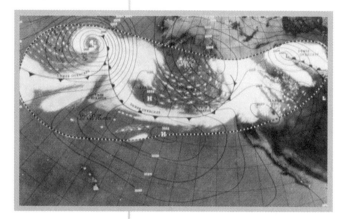

TIROS (Television Infrared Observation Satellite) sent back this map of a North Pacific storm system in May 1960.

An Eye on the Visible— and Invisible—World

In 1945, 12 years before tiny *Sputnik*, the first satellite, was launched, a science-fiction writer named Arthur C. Clarke wrote a plan for using satellites to send radio, TV, and telephone signals. His communication system would bring together people from all the "corners" of the globe. Fifty years later, his wild imaginings had become reality.

Landsat satellites have been circling Earth since *Landsat 1* rode a Delta rocket into orbit in 1972. Landsat was the first of many remote-sensing satellites to put together a big picture of Earth that told many different stories about it. The first maps based on Landsat data completely changed how people saw the world and what they thought about it.

Landsat maps have helped people living on an African prairie recognize that the healthiest part of the prairie was an area where animals were not allowed to eat all the grass. They showed Arctic ships the easiest path to take through the polar ice. They showed parts of the ocean where people were illegally dumping acid. They showed earthquake faults, forest fires, icebergs, glaciers,

The IKONOS (a word derived from the Greek word for "image") satellite took this one-meter resolution image of Sydney, Australia, during the 2000 Olympic Games. From 423 miles above Earth, IKONOS zoomed in so tight that things just one meter wide can be seen.

The first photo taken by a person in space showed North Africa, the first landmass flown over by most spaceships that take off from Cape Canaveral. John Glenn used a drugstore camera, which he had to talk NASA into letting him take along.

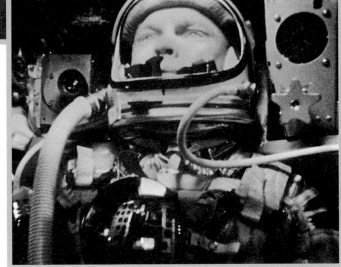

In 1962, John Glenn became the first American to orbit Earth—and to take a picture of it.

mountains, and lakes that nobody knew were there before. Such satellite discoveries were like a brand-new story about the world that had never been told before. For once, explorers were making discoveries about places they had never been.

Landsat and other satellites that came after it were equipped with multiband spectrographs, sensors that identified different kinds of waves. They send the data to Earth, where computers use it to figure out what the waves tell them about the land.

The human eye sees three bands of light: red, green, and blue. The multispectral Landsat cameras record six bands of light, including infrared, heat energy produced by wildlife such as plants. Computers zip the data into GIS systems and out come maps that show the satellite data spread across a geographical area—anything from a city block to a whole country to the whole globe.

Closer to the ground, scientists riding helicopters experiment with *hyperspectral* cameras that show 128 bands of light. This lets the camera pick up incred-

Landsat took this 25-meter resolution image of Mount Rainier, Washington. Color was added to the image to make it a clearer relief map of the area.

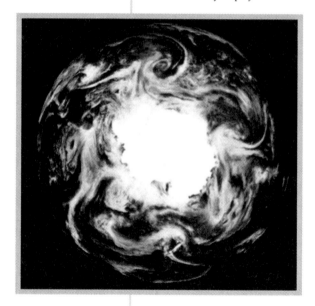

Nobody risked frostbite to gather the images necessary to make this map of Antarctica. The 1997 map was put together like a puzzle or mosaic out of several images taken by the satellite Galileo. Even if Galileo had been precisely over the South Pole to take one picture, half of it would have been dark.

ible amounts of information about a piece of land it focuses on: woods, minerals, gases, liquids, and so forth. What's more, it can zero in on individual trees and compare them to see which are healthiest—something that might be impossible for someone on the ground standing next to the tree to determine.

A little higher up, at 70,000 feet, NASA (National Aeronautics and Space Administration) tests an even more powerful camera from top-secret spy planes. Airborne Visible Infrared Imaging Spectrometer (AVIRIS) cameras can record 224 bands of light. In the early 2000s, these cameras will catch a ride on satellites, too. The maps that result should be spectacular. Or should that be . . . *spectra*cular?

The Problem of Making Maps

The speed of a satellite depends on its altitude. The highest satellites are in *geosynchronous orbit*, which means that they travel at almost the same speed as the earth turns (about 1,000 miles per hour). They seem to hover over one spot and can "watch" that spot. To stay in position, they orbit 23,000 miles above Earth. Lower satellites orbit at different speeds. As Earth turns, one spot on it may move in and out of range of different satellites. This allows one satellite doing one kind of job to do that job around the globe.

Like aerial photographs, these observations aren't maps—but they're used to make maps. With new technology came new problems. The biggest problem for satellites was how to make correct maps.

There have always been problems with making realistic maps. First, there was the problem of measuring a piece of land correctly for a flat map. The answer to that was surveying.

Then there was the problem of making a flat map out of a round world. The answer to that was using projections.

Then came the problem of being in the air above that round world taking a

MAPMAKERS

Danniel and Jackson Maio

"I love New York City," says Jackson Maio. He and his brother Danniel created The Living Map, which covers the East and West sides of Manhattan in detail.

The Maios began with a base map of the area, then visited every block several times. So what makes it a *living* map? "We focus on the people in the neighborhood—where they go, where they shop—information a person living in the neighborhood would use. We did a comprehensive survey store to store, person to person, to bring to the surface what's special about these neighborhoods." What they found often surprised them. "First, the hospital industry was extremely strong," says Danniel. Another discovery was that there are many more riverside activities on the East side than on the West. "People were crabbing, catching healthy crabs. So we put a crab on the map."

The Maio brothers

What seemed like strange behavior by New Yorkers often told a story. "We noticed that a lot of people who ran in Central Park looked down while they ran. When we asked them why, we discovered that there are distance markers painted there, but they're very hard to see, so they had to look closely. We duplicated the distance markers on our map."

They included information that only a neighborhood insider would know: which subway stations are open around the clock, which religion each temple or church is, even which garbage cans are used by which building.

It took the two men four years to cover an area that included 20,000 buildings. Their next goal: to map all of Manhattan. "We want to leave a record," says Danniel. "If we're going to be here on Earth, what can we leave that civilization can benefit from? Certainly, a map will live longer than we will."

flat picture. The answer to that was in matching coordinates. If you knew just what your Global Position was in the air, you could match it with the Global Position on the ground.

Now imagine that you're above the round world, going around it yourself, and taking a flat picture. How can you make your flat picture match up to a flat map? The first part of the answer is to trace a *ground track*—the path where a map's scale was true, directly under the satellite on the ground. The second part of the answer is to design a map projection that matches up with the ground track even though the satellite moves. In 1978, a chemical engineer, John P. Snyder, figured

Remember, a photograph is not a map. But this space shuttle view of Puerto Rico shows things in a new way.

So how do you use the space shuttle to improve on maps? With SRTM, which stands for Shuttle Radar Topography Map. As the shuttle orbits Earth, a boom 200 feet long extending from the cargo bay points radar instruments at Earth.

out the math to make this projection, the Space Oblique Mercator projection. To cartographers, Snyder is a hero for solving the trickiest map problem of the space age.

Seeing Is Believing

And what about our human satellites? I mean astronauts, of course, people who get to fly around Earth once every 90 minutes for a few days (seeing the sun rise and set each time), looking out one of the space shuttle's 11 windows whenever they can.

Space shuttle astronauts are often assigned to study specific parts of the earth for specific information, depending on what researchers on the ground want to find out. Scientists can request photographs from 1,800 observation sites, and astronauts will snap pictures when they reach those points.

Now that pictures have been taken from space for more than 40 years, several shots of one point on Earth can be compared with one another and with maps of the area to draw new conclusions about change. Space shots taken from shuttles flying 180 miles up have helped people see changing patterns in population, farming, pollution, and many other features: the growing Sahara desert, the shrinking rain forest, the thinning Arctic ice, the spread of light pollution, and much, much more.

Now the space shuttle is helping to produce a new view of Earth, SRTM (Shuttle Radar Topography Map). In February 2000, astronauts on the shuttle *Endeavour* aimed a camera

MAPMAKER

Patrick Meyer

By spring 2002, Patrick Meyer, aeronautical engineer at Marshall Space Flight Center in Huntsville, Alabama, will have plotted the positions and courses of 800 satellites. Some are visible to the naked eye: the Hubble telescope, the Mir space station (soon to be de-orbited, Meyer says), and the international space station (under construction in orbit), which will be the size of a football field when it's assembled.

You can get an idea of how these satellites are laid out around Earth by clicking on the NASA website Meyer designed: liftoff.msfc.nasagov/RealTime/JTrack/3D. Click on a dot and you'll find out what the object is, where it is at the moment you click, and the orbital path it's following. These days more than 8,600 human-made satellites are in orbit along with the moon and asteroids. They include "space trash" like gloves lost by astronauts working outside the space shuttle, dead satellites, and live satellites that do everything from tracking the weather to relaying telephone conversations from one side of the world to another.

All sorts of different business and research organizations and governments pay to build satellites, blast them into orbit, and keep track of them. Meyer's map helps them. Soon he hopes to launch new sites to help people learn about the sky above them. "You'll put in your zip code, and we'll show you what the sky above you should look like: night stars, constellations, even satellites passing by."

Try kids.msfc.nasa.gov/sky/jpath/ for more about satellites.

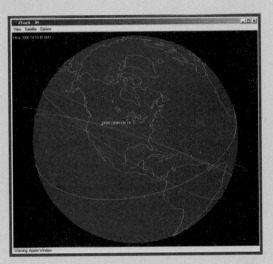

White dots stand for satellites. Zero in on one at the Web site to find out more.

hung from a 200-foot boom extending from the ship's cargo bay toward Earth, gathering information that would be used to map 75 percent of Earth's surface, with more to be added later. Radar was used to take multiple "data pictures" of nearly 50 million square miles of Earth. The data—enough to fill 13,500 CDs—were combined to create a 3-D map of the world, the best-ever, highest-resolution, farthest-reaching topographical map of Earth. It took two years to make a digital map from all the information the shuttle found.

The 3-D map has hundreds of uses, including plant, soil, and animal research, city planning, and flight planning for pilots. Anyone who needs to know the lay of the land for any reason can make use of such a map. Like all topographic maps, it will help the military, too, as they plan training and opera-

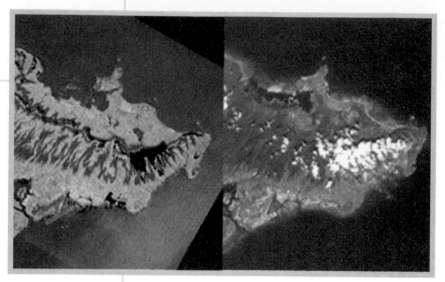

Here are two examples of the kind of detailed relief map SRTM technology provides—one in false color, one in true color (including clouds). That's Honolulu, Hawaii.

SRTM data lets mapmakers create perspective (side) views of land— from a 21st-century bird's-eye view. That space shuttle is some bird!

tions, or in case of battle. Like most of the new technology developed for mapping during the 20th century and before, it was partly built on ideas developed for military use. Military leaders have sometimes been the first to perfect new technology, and they have sometimes kept their findings top secret. It has taken time for the military to free up maps and map technology so that civilians (nonmilitary people, including scientists) could use them. One such technology is high-resolution satellite imagery. Powerful cameras mounted on spy satellites 400 miles above Earth can zero in on land and buildings in close detail. Things just three feet wide will show up in the pictures, and can be included on maps.

Some people argue that only the military should be allowed to see things this closely, so that they can keep a close eye on anyone who might threaten national security. Some say either nobody should—or everybody should. How do you feel about technology so refined that cameras can look in your bathroom window? And if that technology is available, should it be available to anyone who wants it? How much detail is too much detail for a remote sensor to be able to pick up from Earth's orbit? People have gotten used to the idea of having an eye in the sky—or have they?

Photographs of Earth from space have the power to make people cry, they seem so beautiful and amazing. Astronaut Franklin Chang Diaz talks about how fragile Earth's atmosphere seems. Seeing it from space, he says, helped him under-

Should a satellite be able to look closely at things below? The one that took this high-resolution image of the pyramids of Egypt can.

stand how important it was to take care of this system that keeps us all alive on planet Earth.

Getting off the ground and looking back—and applying all the newest technology—lets people see clearly what they could only dream of before—that Earth is all one giant system of land, water, air, and life. Where before we were looking mostly at the shape of lands and oceans, now we're looking deeper. We can see how it all works together. Remote sensing, on-the-ground research, and new ways of mapping have changed the way we look at Earth, forever.

CHAPTER 5

Mapping System Earth

A big globe hangs from the ceiling of the Hall of Planet Earth in the American Museum of Natural History in New York. As the globe turns, it changes. The earth rotates, and clouds fade away to reveal oceans and continents. Then the oceans dry up, and the plants and trees on the land disappear. You can see the bare shape of the land, the deep and deeper levels of the ocean floor. This is the earth, stripped of its atmosphere, its water, and its life.

I sat under this twirling globe for an hour and listened to what museum visitors had to say about it. "Look! There's our house!" They were awed, they were thrilled, and they all did the same thing: They looked for the part of the earth where they lived.

"There's my home!"

This terrific animated globe was created from images from several different satellites. The first view—of the earth with clouds—was copied from a U.S. Air Force weather satellite shot. The shape of the oceans and continents comes from a NOAA (National Oceanic and Atmospheric Administration) Very High Resolution Satellite. The view of the land stripped of vegetation came from a soil map created from satellite data. Satellite data and shipboard depth measurements let the museum create a clear picture of the ocean floor.

Incredible as the globe is at showing how the air, land, plant life, and ocean combine to form planet Earth, everybody who sees it remembers proudly that they live there, too. Hundreds of years ago, it was enough to understand your immediate surroundings. But today people are aware not just that they're New Yorkers or Americans, but that they're Earthlings.

Understanding just how the system we call Earth works is what the newest research, and the maps it leads to, are all about. Getting off the ground and looking back—and applying all the newest technology—has let us see more clearly what we could only dream of before. Before we were looking mostly at the shape of lands and the shores of oceans. Now we're looking deeper.

NASA's ESE (Earth Science Enterprise), launched in 1991, links satellites, a special data system, and scientists who interpret the data. Along with other groups in the United States and around the world, ESE works to understand the weather, the oceans, glaciers and polar ice, the solid earth, the land surface, the atmosphere, energy, and the different ecosystems that interact to make the big ecosystem that is Earth.

The first step in each area of study is to observe what actually happens over the seasons and eventually over the years. New questions lead to new research. As soon as they find out about one thing, it makes them wonder how something else contributes. What causes an earthquake in Japan? Why can the earthquake be felt in the Indian Ocean? How does an erupting volcano in the Philippines change the weather elsewhere? How does the earth work? By using computers to combine research on the ground with satellite views, people are creating maps that show us what maps have always shown—a new world.

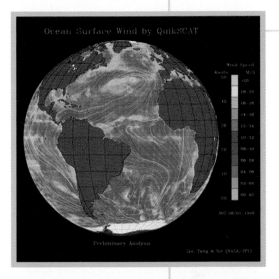

Why the Sky Is Blue

Before weather satellites went into orbit, regular weather observations were available for only one fifth of the globe. In 1959, the satellite *Explorer VI* sent back the first television pictures from space. They showed . . . *ta-da!* . . . clouds. Weather-spotting has always been a major goal of NASA satellites. TIROS (Television Infrared Observation Satellite), the first weather satellite, was launched in 1960. TIROS was only 42 inches wide and 19 inches tall. It flew 400 miles high for just 78 days, circling Earth every 98 minutes. But the information it sent back changed weather prediction forever. In 1965, 450 TIROS images fitted together to become the first global picture of the world's weather.

"Who has seen the wind?" wrote poet Christina Rosetti. The answer: Seasat mappers. Seasat 1 recorded the wind speed at the surface of the oceans, and the data was used to make these maps.

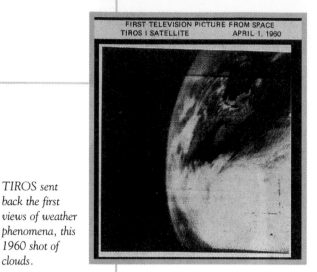

TIROS sent back the first views of weather phenomena, this 1960 shot of clouds.

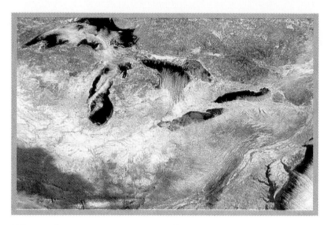

The weather was just as stormy in the 1990s as in the 1960s. But satellite data make for better predictions—and save lives and property. This bit of weather is a blizzard.

Now forecasters have the whole world in their hands by touching a button. New data leads to new questions. It's not "Why is the sky blue?" anymore, but "What is the sky?" and "What happens at different levels of the sky?" and "Does the sky change?" Changes in the sky are what weather satellites are there to notice. Many different low-orbiting TIROS satellites went up after the first. They scanned the atmosphere, picking up changes at different levels, and feeding their findings to scientists on the ground, who used what they learned to map the atmosphere.

In 1975, the first GOES (Geostationary Operational Environmental Satellite) went into orbit. Traveling at 22,300 miles high, it orbited in sync with Earth's rotation. This let its big eye "stare" at one spot on Earth to keep watch on what was happening there, weather-wise. Today a system of GOES keeps the globe covered. A stream of information from GOES feeds into the weather maps that help people plan what to wear and what to do every day.

Up in the Air

There's more to mapping the sky than predicting weather. Mapping the atmosphere has let us figure out the *why* of the weather—as well as the *why* of our climate. A spaceship traveling through the atmosphere can measure what it finds, but a satellite sitting above a specific place—orbiting at a steady level—can really get to know the place. Atmospheric research translates into maps that show what exists at each of the sky's four layers, and how each layer affects the weather and climate.

By measuring the temperature, flow, and makeup of the air at different layers, scientists figured out what went on there. In the stratosphere, for example, jet streams form quick-moving rivers of air. Stronger in winter, they tend to flow in predictable patterns. They help determine the climate. By studying what the jet streams are doing, people can make better predictions about the weather.

People study the ozone layer from the ground as well as from satellites. The ozone layer absorbs harmful ultraviolet rays from the sun. During the early 1980s, a team studying the ozone layer from Antarctica noticed that ozone levels were dropping. Meanwhile, a satellite called TOMS (Total Ozone Mapping Spectrometer) was checking the ozone. TOMS was designed to make maps, but there was one major problem with it. The computer was programmed to throw out any data that fell outside what the programmers expected the ozone level to be. So the computer was mapping the ozone layer wrong.

The Antarctica scientists produced a graph showing what their results had been. People were surprised, but nobody paid much attention. So the team asked for a new map from TOMS, including all the data that TOMS found. The result was a map that stunned the world. It showed a hole in the ozone layer over Antarctica, one that had formed as the result of pollution.

The map created a huge debate over what was happening to the ozone layer, and whether it could harm the world. And people began talking about ways to reverse what was happening. TOMS also shows what happens to the climate in the short term, such as the clouds that shaded much of the world after Mt. Pinatubo erupted in the Philippines in 1991. Other satellites chime in to help

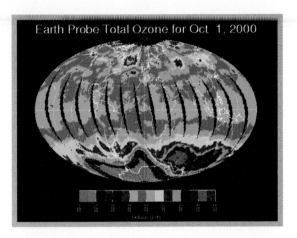

Earth Probe Total Ozone for Oct 1, 2000

Dr. Richard McPeters, who monitors the ozone hole above Antarctica, figures that this map shows the ozone hole, in red, at its worst—or nearly largest—level. It could take 30 years or longer for the ozone layer to recover. Compare the hole on October 1, 2000, with . . .

Earth Probe Total Ozone for Oct 1, 1999

. . . the ozone hole on October 1, 1999.

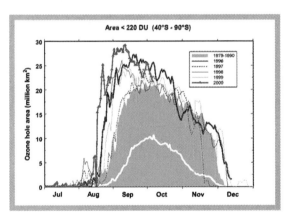

Area < 220 DU (40°S - 90°S)

Do numbers add up to a hole? With the ozone layer, they did. The ozone graph proves it: Maps rule!

predict weather changes caused by climate patterns such as El Niño and La Niña. On a daily basis, all kinds of satellites pick up all kinds of information about the atmosphere. They link with mapping computers to provide the weather maps that appear on the television weather forecasts or in the newspaper daily.

Questions Lead to Maps Lead to Questions Lead to . . .

New maps, new questions. It was Sir Francis Bacon, a 17th-century English philosopher, who first commented on how the eastern coast of South America would fit into the western coast of Africa. He was looking at a map when he thought of it.

In 1912, Alfred Wegener argued that the continents were not stuck in place but had moved, and were still moving. There had once been a supercontinent, he said, and he named it Pangaea. Wegener's theory said that Pangaea had drifted apart, and its pieces—called plates—plowed through oceans, crashed into other landmasses, and created new landforms, like mountain ranges, through sheer force. He went so far as to give evidence of the similarities in plants and rock types in South America and Africa that showed they had once been closer together.

Wegener's theory was called *plate tectonics*. But Wegener had trouble convincing other scientists, who asked what made the plates move.

The answer lay at the bottom of the ocean.

In 1854, Matthew Maury of the U.S. Navy made the first map of the North Atlantic ocean floor by dropping down a weighted line and measuring how far

It was a map of the world that first gave Sir Francis Bacon the idea that the continents were like puzzle pieces that had spread apart from one another. This map shows some of the plates—giant pieces of the earth's crust—that the continents sit on during their slow, slow shift over the globe.

it fell. *Sonar*—the practice of bouncing sound waves off solid objects to determine their shape and distance—was discovered in the 1920s. It's similar to the method bats and dolphins use to find their way and to find food, and scientists used it to find the depth of the ocean at specific places. In the 1940s and 1950s, a group of scientists at Columbia University used new sonar readings to confirm the long, thin, underwater mountain chain that Maury had "seen" a century earlier. Maurice Ewing and Bruce Heezen used shipboard sonar to find islands underwater just where they thought Maury's mid-Atlantic ridge should be. They hadn't measured the ridge completely yet, but they felt that the islands were evidence that it was there. What's more, the ridge wasn't just a chain of mountains. There was a valley down the middle of them, a rift as if the mountains were being pulled apart. Ewing and Heezen's teammate, Marie Tharp, used the findings to paint a map of the ocean floor, using false color to show the different levels.

MAPS MAKE THE DIFFERENCE

Frank I. González

Frank I. González maps tsunamis, tidal waves that can sweep across the ocean.

Frank González is an oceanographer at the Pacific Marine Laboratory in Seattle. He's working on two different kinds of mapping involving tsunamis, powerful and dangerous waves. The first is mapping that tracks the path of the tsunami from the place where it starts to coastline areas where it might wash ashore. The second kind of mapping helps people onshore figure out just which areas might be flooded by a tsunami and which will be safe.

"The only way to be sure whether a wave is headed toward a distant coast is to place tsunami detectors in its path and track it across the open ocean," says González. Tsunamis usually begin at the site of an underwater earthquake, volcanic eruption, or landslide. Because the Pacific Ocean is such a hotbed of moving plates, most tsunamis happen there. González is part of a NOAA team that is developing a network of six deep-ocean reporting stations—buoys that measure changes in the ocean waves.

Tsunamis travel relatively slowly in the deep ocean. As they near shore, they speed up, because the energy they contain builds up in a smaller area. The buoys pick up information about the size and speed of a wave, and send data that can be coordinated with an ocean map to show just where the tsunami is, in what direction it's moving, and how big it is—which give scientists clues to how powerful it will be when it makes landfall.

The Columbia team kept working to map the ocean, and by 1956, they said that the mid-Atlantic rift wasn't just in the mid-Atlantic. It ran, they said, down the Atlantic, south of Africa, up the Indian Ocean, and across the Pacific. It was the largest structure on Earth, a mountain range running 40,000 miles. What's more, they said that the rift was a seam marking the area where Earth's hot mantle oozed through to form a crust that grew and changed, "a wound that never heals."

We're not talking blood here. We're talking red-hot lava. Lava, said Princeton scientist Harry Hess, paves the ocean floor where the ridges are—and causes the seafloor to spread. The continents, he said, moved on top of the sheets of ocean crust. This movement caused underwater volcanoes and earthquakes.

More proof of the plate tectonics theory came from two different sources: a bird's-eye view and a fish's-eye view. Scientist J. Tuzo Wilson was flying over the Hawaiian Islands when he noticed that the islands toward the east were less eroded (worn down) and seemed newer (younger) than the western ones. Hawaii, he said, rode on the Pacific plate. As it moved over a hot spot in Earth's mantle, a volcanic island would erupt, building up until it burst through the ocean's surface. That's what Wilson guessed from above.

Down below, geophysicists Fred Vine and Drummond Matthews used a magnetometer to find magnetic stripes on the ocean floor. Some stripes near the coast of California, they found, were cut short. On further study, they determined that the stripes weren't missing, but had gone underground, as the Pacific plate slipped beneath the edge of North America.

The Closest Frontier: The Ocean Floor

Only 5 percent of the ocean floor has been studied, compared to 100 percent of the surface of the moon. How is that possible, when the moon is far away, and the ocean is close at hand? In a way, the moon is easier to get at. You can see it; it's not covered up by anything like a googol of gallons of water. Seventy percent of the earth is ocean. That means 70 percent of the earth's surface is sitting where we can't see it—bird's-eye view or not.

Before the late 1970s, soundings and magnetometer readings could be taken only directly under a boat. Then came *Seasat*. In 1978, *Seasat* was the first satellite that could do remote sensing of the ocean. It collected data about sea-surface temperature, wave heights, wave lengths and direction, sea ice, and ocean topography. Yes, topography. Could *Seasat* see through the ocean to the hills and valleys of the ocean floor? In an odd way, it could.

Seasat measured gravity anomalies, places where the earth's gravity varied. Here's how it works: The sea seems flat, but actually it has hills and valleys. They correspond with what's under the surface. If there's a valley on the seafloor, the ocean surface dips. If there's a mountain, it rises. And the gravity level differs along with the shape of the ocean floor.

Columbia University scientist William Haxby took the 14 computer tapes *Seasat*

A shallow, sandy bottom is no problem for boats in Ocean City, Maryland, thanks to a map that shows what things are like underwater. Satellite measurements have made nautical charts like this much more accurate than they used to be.

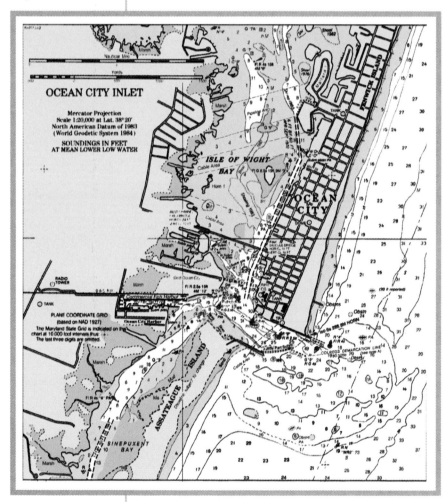

produced and plotted them, connecting data from each place with that place on a world map. Haxby used colors to represent different levels, and spread each colored point across a map. The result was a rainbow picture that seemed to be the shape of the ocean floor—although really it was the shape of the ocean surface. And what a picture it was. There in perfect relief were the ocean's ridges, showing up like patchwork seams, marking where the dozen plates fit together. When William Haxby mapped the ocean floor, John L. LaBrecque, another scientist, said, "It was like he had drained the water out of the ocean."

Satellite technology has made it possible for scientists to peek through the water and get a glimpse of the ocean floor. It would have taken a sonar ship 142 years to cover the same territory that *Seasat* covered. In 1985, *Geosat*, flying with instruments twice as sensitive as *Seasat*'s, made a map so detailed that at first it was top secret.

Once the data was released, scientists found a new mystery. The most unexpected data came from the Weddell Sea at the tip of the South American plate and the Antarctic plate. No other ocean floor looks like this one, which is described as looking like fish bones. The structures down there arose

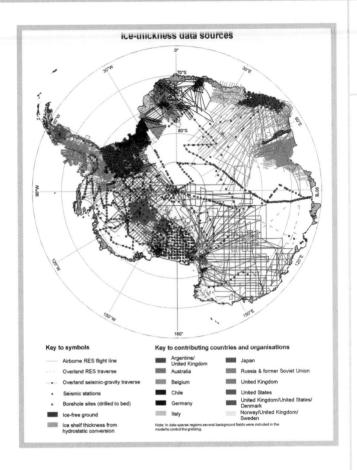

The different colored lines on this map each stand for the research findings of a country that studied the thickness of the ice in Antarctica. All these countries worked as part of the BEDMAP consortium. Put their data together and . . .

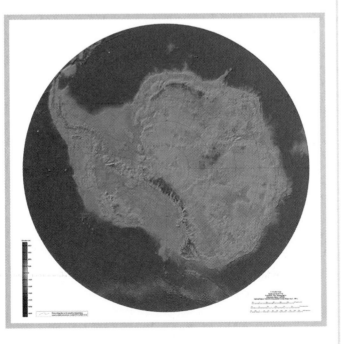

. . . you get a relief map (called the BEDMAP topographic map because it maps the ice bed elevation) of Antarctica, in which different colors stand for different thicknesses and elevations of ice.

MAPS MAKE THE DIFFERENCE

Dana Yoerger

Dana Yoerger is an oceanographic engineer at the Woods Hole Oceanographic Institute (WHOI) in Cape Cod, Massachusetts. He works to design and build submarines—manned and robotic—that can drop to the ocean floor and find stuff. What kind of stuff? The *Titanic*, for one. The WHOI submarine *Jason* took *Titanic* hunters to the floor of the North Atlantic to find the sunken ship.

Other amazing stuff includes the deep vents (cracks) in the ocean floor, places where lava plumes billow high. Sub *Alvin* took people down to look at those plumes. Sub *ABE* went on its own, with WHOI scientists at the remote controls, and took pictures of what Yoerger calls the Crack of Doom. Now Yoerger is working on *ABE II*, which will be able to take instruments under water to explore, gather data, and map as never before.

Mapping the ocean is important, Yoerger says. It might be more important to focus on certain parts of the ocean in detail. "In some parts of the ocean there isn't a whole lot going on." Where would he zero in? Juan de Fuca Sound, off the coast of British Columbia, for one. "Watching the vents there change with time is an issue the whole scientific community is interested in. If we can find the part that will teach us the most important science lessons, to me that's why we want to do mapping."

100 million years ago, scientists say. But nobody knows—yet—what happened then to make them so different from everywhere else.

In the year 2000, 14 new relief maps made from SRTM data (see Chapter 4) showed detailed surfaces and seabeds of the earth more accurately than ever before. No longer top secret, and no longer invisible, the ocean floor is our new frontier, and scientists everywhere are itching to explore it.

Which Came First, the Fish or the Fish Egg?

One thing's for certain: The first life came from the ocean. Researchers using submarines, ships, satellites, and the latest maps can locate and explore the cracks in the deep ocean floor. These "smokestacks" ooze lava that mixes with ocean water to make watery smoke. The new life thriving around them is an important clue to just how life formed in the early days of Earth. Mapmakers can put the research findings into maps—maps that raise questions about how life on Earth might change in the future.

The ocean floor holds clues to all the things that lived in the oceans in the past—as well as to the earth's climate hundreds and thousands and millions of years ago. So does plain old dirt in the backyard, and so does ice at the North and South poles. By combining what they find there, scientists are putting together maps that show what the climate was like in those places in the past. They're also creating models that show what the climate and weather—and the life on planet Earth—will be like in the future.

Change one, and watch the others change like dominos tumbling in a row. What would happen, for example, if the hole in the ozone layer grew and Earth's temperature rose? How much would the polar ice melt? How much would ocean levels rise as a result of melting ice? What shores would be underwater as a result of rising oceans? What life would thrive, and what would fail? The model begins as a stack of math problems: If this number changed, what would that number do?

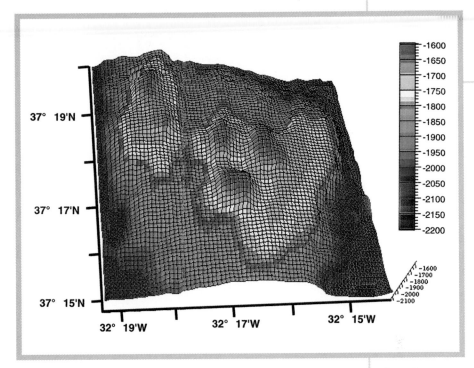

A computer turns numbers into shapes in this digital contour map, which shows the elevation of the ocean floor.

What a relief! A color system linked to depths and elevations found by satellites helped create this world map. (It's a Mercator projection, by the way.)

MAPMAKER
Tanya Atwater

Tanya Atwater creates maps that are movies to show how Earth's plates move, creating rifts, faults, and earthquakes.

Tanya Atwater, professor of geology at the University of California at Santa Barbara, creates animated films showing how earthquakes are created along the San Andreas Fault in California. The films squeeze millions of years into a few seconds of movements.

Q. What is the San Andreas Fault?
A. Here in western North America we're on two huge plates—the Pacific plate and the North American plate. The San Andreas Fault is the big boundary. These plates are going by each other and scraping each other, shattering and reorganizing the land. They're pulling it apart to make big basins and smashing pieces together to make tall mountains, twirling places around to make the coastlines go in different directions.

Q. Why did you make a movie map of this?
A. Geology is so slow-moving. On a human time-scale it's hard to imagine what the plates are doing. Geologists tend to be pretty good at having little mental movies, to imagine the earth moving, the mountains growing. We have good visual imaginations. When we try to explain what we think we see in our own minds, we're always waving our arms, trying to make our pictures move.

Q. How did you make your pictures into an animation?
A. At first, I was always trying to make flip books. But as soon as I animated my flip books I immediately saw things I'd done wrong. So I redid the maps, using Photoshop images and an animation program called Morph.

To see Atwater's animations, check out her Web site at www.geol.ucsb.edu/~atwater/Animations.

Mapping the Earth's Plates: A Moving Experience

Earth is estimated to be 4.5 billion years old. Over time, *everything* has moved and changed. There are fracture zones all over the floor of the ocean to mark where the plates have spread apart.

The floor of the Indian Ocean has ridges like corduroy, thanks to the weight of the Indian plate as it smashed into the subcontinent. The Himalayas, the world's highest mountains, were pushed up because of the pressure of the Indian plate.

The Great Rift is a deep valley in East Africa that runs 2,299 miles from the tip of the Red Sea to Zimbabwe. It is lined with long, narrow lakes 5,000 feet deep. Eventually it could spread as the Red Sea has, to create a new ocean—and make an island of East Africa.

Off the coast of the Pacific Northwest, deep trenches show that the Pacific plate is sliding under North America. Farther south, those two plates have created a crack in the land itself, the famous San Andreas Fault, which may eventually split California the way East Africa is splitting. Under the ocean east of Japan, the world's deepest ocean trenches are more evidence that one plate is sliding over another.

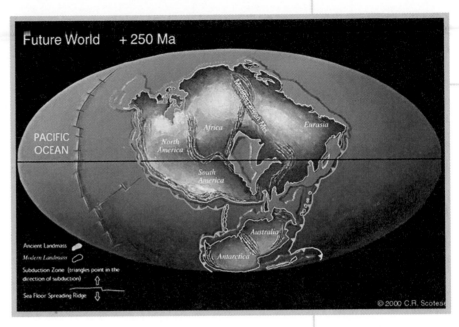

Almost all the world's major earthquakes occur around the edges of the Pacific. As lava rises from the center of the Pacific, the seafloor spreads. The continental plates push over the ocean plates. The edges of the continents bordering the Pacific form a "ring of fire" of earthquakes.

Seismic movement is what happens when the plates move. *Seismic tomography* is the study of just what the movement does to the earth—and how it feels to the people on it. Scientists can not only map what movement takes place under the ground, but they can use seismic tomography to figure out just what is under the ground.

Seismic tomographers have a global network of seismic stations that allows them to map inner planet Earth. The stations sit ready and waiting for earthquakes, and when they come, they measure how long it takes for the waves to travel. This allows them to keep track of and map what's happening far, far underground.

Inside the earth, the rock moves and flows, changing from solid to liquid and back again at certain places called the CMB (core-mantle boundary). The CMB, tomographers have learned, tends to create "hot spots" in the surface above it. This is where you'll find hot springs, geysers, and active volcanoes.

How do you show this on a map? With false color. Seismic tomographers Adam Dziewonski and John Woodhouse linked orange with areas where the liquid core was rising toward the surface, and blue with cooler areas where the mantle was sinking down. The result was a map that helped people to clearly see the underground causes of events happening on the earth's surface.

Chris Scotese imagined how the earth's plates might move over the next 250 million years, if they continue in their current pattern, and he drew a map to match his prediction.

What's inside the earth?

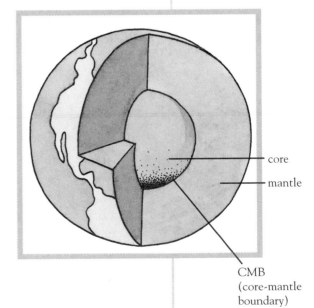

core

mantle

CMB (core-mantle boundary)

Mapping You

Scientists map people and animals, too. In the Arctic, they used tags and GPS to trace endangered peregrine falcons—and their work helped bring the falcons back from the edge of extinction. Along the ocean coasts, the same kind of system helps track sea turtles, in hope of learning enough about their complicated migration patterns to help them build up their numbers.

Meanwhile, in America, two grandfathers invented global positioning monitors so they could put satellites to work keeping track of their grandchildren. It's a safety measure, they say, one they hope to sell to other people who want to know where someone is. With the combination of GPS and maps, it's easy to follow anyone or anything.

What else can you do with GPS? Play Geocaching, a GPS treasure hunt game. Someone hides a treasure, and uses a handheld GPS monitor to find the exact position of the treasure. (Imagine if old-time pirates had had GPS: They wouldn't have needed an X to mark the spot of the treasure on their maps!) Others use their GPS monitors to home in on the treasure. Check out www.geocaching.com for more.

Some water parks have begun issuing GPS monitors to kids who use the parks. When you buy your ticket, you get an instrument that you wear like a wristwatch. A computer keeps track of your whereabouts through GPS signals—and can find you if you're missing.

So we can even map individuals. But if you haven't got a GPS monitor, you can still find yourself on many maps—maps that show information about people.

GPS monitors keep kids safe at water parks—and allow everything from falcons and sea turtles to gorillas and people to be monitored as they move around the earth.

Cartographers use statistics about everything from how many people there are in an area to how many Spanish-speakers, ice-cream eaters, power boaters, ice skaters, or guinea-pig owners there are. In the 21st century, if you can find information, you can map it, no matter what part of the planet it comes from.

Scientists from America and Rwanda, an African country, are putting their heads—and their tools—together to help gorillas in the Virunga conservation area. There are about 320 gorillas in all, representing more than half of all the gorillas in the world. Yes, these animals are endangered. But the work people are doing here could help.

On the ground, humans keep track of where gorillas are, using GPS units that "talk" to satellites to pinpoint their location. From space, remote sensors on satellites study the soil and plants below, using instruments so detailed they can figure out where the plants gorillas love—things like stinging nettles and wild celery—are located. The sensors can also find paths through wilderness areas, campsites where poachers might hide to hunt gorillas, and places where the forest has been destroyed. On the computer, scientists use GIS. They layer their findings over topographical maps, space shuttle photographs of the area, and other data to create maps that show where gorillas thrive.

Where would you live if you were a gorilla? Satellites and planes help mappers figure out where gorilla habitats in Rwanda are—and how to improve conditions in that country for both gorillas and humans.

There are other things in Rwanda that could be built up through mapping besides the gorilla population. That's just the first goal. War-torn Rwanda needs help deciding on new ways to use land and to find and use natural resources. Maps such as the gorilla maps could help.

CHAPTER 6

Look Out! A Whole Lot of Space

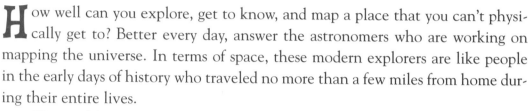

How well can you explore, get to know, and map a place that you can't physically get to? Better every day, answer the astronomers who are working on mapping the universe. In terms of space, these modern explorers are like people in the early days of history who traveled no more than a few miles from home during their entire lives.

We Earthlings don't really know where we are in relation to the whole pile of stars and space. We don't know whether we have any living neighbors. We don't know how high or long or wide the cosmos is. We have no real idea of the limits of our universe—or if there's any end to it at all.

Throughout history, people have come up with theories about how the universe came to be, how big it is, and how it works. Just as there seems to be no end to the universe we can see, there is no end to the questions being explored by *cosmologists* (people who study the cosmos or the universe) and *astronomers* (people who study the stars).

How big is the universe? Every year more and more stars and galaxies are discovered and named, making cosmologists think that we're nowhere close to the edge yet—if there *is* an edge. By using the most modern instruments and probing as deeply as possible into the universe, galaxies of stars 14 billion light-years away have been located. The light waves from those stars took 14 billion years to reach Earth. What we're seeing when we look at them isn't how they look now, it's how they looked 14 billion years ago, when the light started traveling toward us. (Just how long was that? Well, Earth itself is *only* 4.5 billion years old.)

The universe began, many scientists say, when a "cosmic egg" of energy exploded in an event called the Big Bang, setting off a chain reaction that created star after star after star. Stars are still flying away from the center of that explosion, whole galaxies of stars traveling at incredible speeds. How long ago was that? Our best guess about the age of the universe is 14 billion years, because that's the age of the farthest galaxies we know about. Most likely the universe is younger than 20 billion years. If we find more stars farther away, our idea of the age of the universe will change.

Satellite Clementine took this photo of Earth and the moon.

MAPMAKER

Charles Liu

Charles Liu is an astro-physicist at the American Museum of Natural History in New York City.

Imagine mapping every-thing, all at once. In his work at the American Museum of Natural History's Rose Center of Astronomy, astro-physicist Charles Liu has tried to do just that.

When you arrive at the Rose Center, the first thing you see is a huge white ball. Is it the earth? the sun? the uni-verse? a cell? an atom? As you walk through the Rose Center's exhibits, you realize that the ball is all these things—and more.

A walk through the Rose Center can be a moving experience in more ways than one. "Where I feel it most is when you get into the microscopic area. As an astrophysicist, I think about big stuff all the time. But when I look at the comparison between a raindrop and a blood cell . . . If the big white ball stands for a raindrop, millions of red blood cells can fit into it—and one is the size of my hand.

"Our basic thinking is that there are big things in the universe and small things in the universe, and they all matter." One goal of the Rose Center exhibits is to help people understand just how massively, enormously huge the universe is—and how tiny the tiniest things are. "From the edge of the universe down to the tiniest cell, the difference in size is 10 to the 42nd power," Liu says. (That's a 1 with 42 zeroes after it. Ask your math teacher for help to understand how big this number is.)

What's the point of mapping such an incredible thing as the universe? Liu's answer is that maps are what people want. "Maps give us a sense of security or purpose, of belonging, of context. It is possible for people to comprehend this kind of scale in size and time. We are never satisfied unless we know exactly where we are and can point to something and say, 'That's where I am.'"

The big white ball at the American Museum of Natural History might stand for the sun . . . or the earth . . . or the human brain . . . or the whole universe. It's a wild way to map, and it works.

New stars and galaxies of stars are being discovered so quickly that *The Guinness Book of World Records* can't keep up. There's always a new record being broken for "Farthest Away Object." No, nobody's been to those "new" stars (yet). But seeing something, or even just the proof that something exists, means that you can map it.

The Universe: A History of Wrong Ideas

First wrong idea: The world ends at the shoreline of the sea around us. *Terra-centrists* put the land (*terra*) at the center.

Second wrong idea: The earth is the center of the solar system. *Geocentrists* put the earth (*geo*) at the center.

Third wrong idea: The sun is the center of the universe. *Heliocentrists* put the sun (*helios*) at the center.

Fourth wrong idea: The Milky Way is the center of the universe. *Galacto-centrists* put our galaxy (*galactos*) at the center.

A realistic idea of our universe has been a long time coming. It has been some 500 years since people realized that Earth wasn't the center of the universe. Most of us were born in the 20th century, the century when people realized that the sun was the center of just our little solar system, not the entire universe.

Our understanding of our place under the sun is very new, and it changes by the minute. While it's true that the ocean under our noses is mostly unexplored, and that we still have loads to learn about our own planet, we can't help looking up at the stars and wondering. In that sense, we're no different from the ancient Babylonians.

It was the Babylonians who divided a circle into 360 degrees, and it was the Babylonians who first divided—and mapped—the circular sky overhead. At first, the sky was divided into quarters according to the brightest stars in the major constellations: Scorpio (the scorpion), Leo (the lion), Taurus (the bull), and Pegasus (the winged horse). The stars corresponded to the four turning points of the year, the beginning of each new season. Eventually each of these quarters was divided in three, so the sky had 12 portions. Each measured 30 degrees and corresponded to a 30-day month.

Those months were linked to horoscopes, precise predictions based on birthdays. To the Babylonians, every aspect of a person's life was determined by the moment that he was born. The heavenly sun, moon, planets, and stars were linked with the earthly elements of fire, earth, air, and water to create a person's soul.

50 B.C.
The Egyptians adopted the Babylonian zodiac (center of wheel) but included their own Decans in this zodiac. The Decans, represented by the figures on the edges of the wheel, stood for 36 points at which the sun rose over the course of the year, another kind of calendar. The Egyptians used the Decans to mark their weeks, which each had ten days. This is the oldest known zodiac.

This idea spread to India, Egypt, Greece, and other cultures. People today still rely on the stars to guide their lives. What's *your* sign?

Numbering the Stars

The ancient Greeks also used the stars to help keep a calendar, but they added something else to their observation of the sky: measurement.

1544
Battista Agnese's map shows how the sky was divided into 12 equal portions, each represented by a zodiac symbol.

The Greeks imagined that the sky was a solid, crystal, see-through globe surrounding the earth. They divided the celestial globe by drawing lines from north to south and east to west. The crisscross lines—the first longitude and latitude lines—allowed them to plot the positions of the stars, much as people can plot their positions on the earth. This idea—called *spherical geometry*—led to the first scientific understanding of the sky. It also led to the first scientific measurements of Earth itself.

The Greeks noticed how the universe rolled—and they rocked on with new theories. In the fourth century B.C., Parmenides figured that Earth was a sphere, and that the moon shone with light reflected from the sun. Empedocles recognized that solar eclipses happened when the moon passed directly between Earth and the sun, blocking the light of the sun. The Greeks realized that circles and spheres were the key to understanding how the heavens worked—or at least that part of the heavens right above Earth.

Around 375 B.C., Eudoxus of Cnidus made the first celestial globe, which showed the position of the stars relative to the earth. He also described how the earth, the sun, the planets, and the moon revolved within that celestial globe.

Turn, Turn, Turn

But what made it all move? Around 350 B.C., Aristotle added to the Greek model, figuring that everything was geared together, a total of 55 spheres that rotated around one another. Only the earth didn't move, Aristotle said; it was too big and heavy.

Try counting the stars some time, and consider how you would go about remembering each star's position. People have been doing this for thousands of years, and are still doing it today. In 150 B.C., Hipparchus, a Greek, developed one of the first *astrolabes,* an instrument for measuring the position of the stars, and began a star catalog. He listed 850 stars and their positions. Around A.D. 150, Ptolemy revised Hipparchus' star catalog, adding almost 200 more stars. These stars—and the 48 constellations the Greeks drew—guided European astronomers right up to the 17th century. But a list of stars wasn't the same as a map.

By the fifth century A.D., Chinese astronomers had a star catalog with 1,464 stars and 284 constellations. A Chinese drawing made in A.D. 940 is the oldest existing star chart, a map that shows the positions of the stars.

940

This Chinese map is the oldest paper star chart. You can see the Big Dipper on the far left.

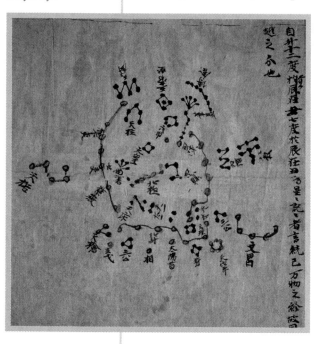

By A.D. 800, astronomers in India used a set of wheels to explain how the heavenly bodies revolved above Earth. During the 800s, the Aztec and Mayan cultures of Central America and South America had a detailed calendar and a system of astronomy based on math, but they didn't try to explain how the stars "moved." Their astronomy was flat, with layers and no spheres.

Between 800 and 1200, Islamic astronomers perfected the astrolabe, an instrument so like a map of the sky that paper maps weren't needed to identify stars. The most famous of these astronomers, Al-Sufi, created *The Book of the Fixed Stars,* which gave his countrymen a better idea of the sky than the Europeans, who still relied on Ptolemy's *Almagest.* By the 13th century, Muslim astronomers had perfected the astrolabe. By the 16th century, astronomers and geographers were working together in an Istanbul observatory, using astrolabes and celestial globes to guide their plotting.

Starry-eyed Dreamers

The Renaissance, a period of great creativity and invention—and mapping—began around 1400, and centered in Italy. For the next 300 years, mapping of Earth and sky sped along, improving as quickly as maps could be drawn. Celestial mapping led the way, because the plotting of coordinates and the projections the Greeks had developed to map the sky helped with earthly mapping, too.

The terrestrial (land) mapper had a harder time than the celestial (sky) mapper. To map the land, you had to represent positions and relations and topographic

features such as hills and lakes and shores. The celestial mapper recorded only positions of the stars. But things did change in the sky, and to have accurate star maps, you had to provide different maps for different times of the year—and the person using your map had to understand that the stars "rose" and "set" the way everything else did, moving across the sky in the course of a night. As with land maps, sky maps were limited by what the mapmakers knew.

As explorers began voyaging around the oceans, they began crying out for better maps, not just of the land and sea, but also of the sky. Along came the printing press, and new maps became possible. People wanted globes, too, and having one became a sign that you were a thinking person. People having their portraits painted often had a globe in their hands or on a nearby table. Knowledge of the world, back then, was a status symbol.

It was a time for big thinking. Among the biggest big thinkers was Copernicus, who thought that the sun was the center of the universe, not Earth. He was wrong about the size of the universe, but he was right about the sun—and his ideas changed how people had thought of their world since time began. Saying that Earth wasn't the most important heavenly body—and that it moved—was sinful to some people, so Copernicus didn't say too much about his idea. It wasn't published until the day he died, in 1543. The proof of his theory—and the person who would fight for it—would come later.

Tycho Brahe, a man from Denmark, disagreed with Copernicus' system. He was wrong about that, but he was right about something else—the star chart he published in 1598 and the celestial globe he designed to go with it. Brahe began a new era of careful, correct positions for stars that were based on observation and

1600

The Blaeu-Golius celestial globe gores. There are two ways to make celestial globes: as if you were looking out from Earth, and as if you were looking in from a point beyond space. How can you tell? Look at Taurus, the bull. If his nose is to the right of his body, you're an extraterrestrial. If his nose points left, you're on Earth. Most celestial globes are made from that extraterrestrial point of view. Compare this view with the one on page 95.

It wasn't easy being an "Astronomer by Candlelight," as this painting by Gerrit Dou shows.

What was between the stars? Thomas Wright created this 1750 view.

measurements. And from these came the first accurate celestial maps.

Science vs. God

At the beginning of the 17th century, Galileo Galilei used one of the first telescopes to prove that Earth did, indeed, move around the sun. He was the first to spy the moons of Jupiter, and he mapped the heavens to include them. Of course, he placed the sun at the center. But the Catholic Church thought it was heresy—a sin against God—to say that Earth wasn't central. The pope brought Galileo to trial, and he was found guilty of going against the beliefs of the church. He spent the rest of his life under house arrest, meaning he wasn't allowed to leave home. It was not until 1992 that the leaders of the Catholic Church pardoned Galileo. By then, the *Galileo* spacecraft had been launched by NASA. It was already heading for Jupiter, to see close up what Galileo had seen only dimly through his telescope.

At around the same time, Johannes Kepler published laws that explained the ways the planets moved around the sun. By the end of the century, Isaac Newton added his understanding of gravity, velocity, and mass—ideas that created the first pure theory of how the cosmos worked and what made it go.

How did the cosmos fit together? New astronomers and celestial cartographers worked in tandem to form new theories and explain them through maps. One of the most original thinkers was Thomas Wright, who stopped mapping stars around 1750 and began drawing models of how he thought the stars might be scattered through space, including other galaxies that were only dreamed of, not discovered. A comet hunter, Charles Messier, identified 109 star clusters, *nebulae* (clouds of stars), and galaxies, as well as named and numbered more than 7,000 stars. Messier was the first to rate the brightness, or *magnitude*, of the stars he named. In 1785, William Herschel was the first to measure the distances between the stars in space. He mapped the Milky Way and realized that the stars in it were grouped into a huge disk formation. Something puzzled him about that disk, though. What was beyond it?

The Sun

Our solar system lies in one arm of the loose spiral galaxy called the Milky Way. Its center is a star—the sun.

Earth orbits the sun at a distance of about 93 million miles. The sun is "just" eight light-minutes away. When we see the sun's light, we see what it looked like eight minutes ago. Research from the ground and from satellites is giving us a closer-than-ever look at our favorite fireball. What the sun does—flaring up, for example—has a great effect on Earth. Where on the sun do these actions occur? And what kinds of effects do they cause?

The TRACE (Transition Region and Coronal Explorer) satellite telescope takes pictures of Earth. Now that TRACE is in orbit, mapmakers will try to use what it finds to map the sun. Reading that map will be the next challenge.

"We have no idea what's going on here," says Edward DeLucca of Harvard-Smithsonian Center for Astrophysics, as he studies TRACE's first look at the sun. "You take these into a room full of scientists and they all say, 'What's that?'" When it comes to astronomy, there's always something new to look at.

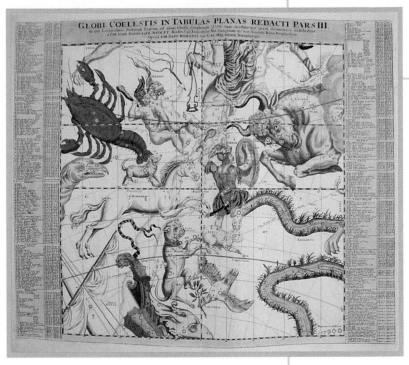

1729
Every line on this map is part of a "great circle," making it practical for navigation.

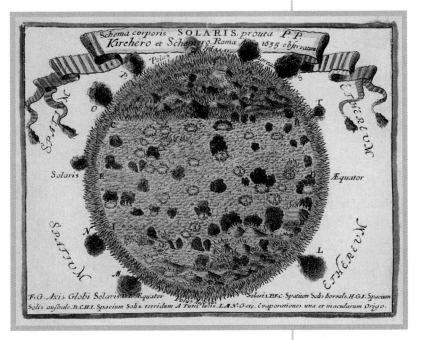

1680
A view of the sun from Seller's Atlas Coelistis (Celestial Atlas) shows early views of sunspots, which could be seen through a telescope.

The Moon

It takes one second for sunlight reflected from the moon to reach Earth. That makes the moon one light-second away, or 864,000 miles. Unlike most other objects in space, our maps of it are based on actual visits, and the moon is 100 percent mapped.

Different views of the planets taken from the Hubble Space Telescope were put together to make this photo map of the solar system.

The Planets

The word *planet* comes from a Greek word meaning "wanderer." To the Greeks, the planets seemed to wander across the sky, unlike the stars, which seemed fixed in place.

Mercury and Venus were first visited by *Mariner 10*. Launched in 1973, it passed Venus in February 1974, and went on to Mercury in March. It was the first spacecraft to use the gravitational pull of one planet—Venus—to push it on to another—Mercury. Venus has been explored and mapped through radar, because clouds cover it from our view.

Everybody wants to go to Mars, our nearest planet, but cost and logistics get in the way. Since the Soviet craft *Marsnik 1* did a flyby in 1960, many missions have set Mars as a goal. *Mariner 4* was the first craft to land there, in November 1964, after a 228-day journey from Earth. The last successful mission to Mars was the Mars Global Surveyor, which mapped the planet in 1997. A manned mission to the nearest planet would cost many billions of dollars.

The *Galileo* mission to Jupiter and its moons was launched in 1989. After a six-year journey, it entered Jupiter's orbit and has been there ever since, photographing and analyzing Jupiter and the four natural satellites discovered in 1610 by the man it's named after.

The *Voyager* missions, launched a month apart in 1977, have explored our solar system and now venture beyond its borders. *Voyager 1* was launched in September 1977. It passed Jupiter in 1979 and Saturn in 1980, then went on past Titan, Saturn's moon, and out of the planets' orbital paths. *Voyager 2* went up a month before *Voyager 1*, and traveled more slowly to Jupiter, then onward to pass Saturn in 1981, Uranus in 1986, and Neptune in 1989. Its travels—nicknamed the "Grand Tour"—reminded some people of Magellan's great journey around the world, except that it sent back postcards. Pictures of the distant planets and Triton,

MAPS MAKE THE DIFFERENCE

Jack and Ben Van Dusen

Jack Van Dusen is a Eugene, Oregon, teacher who worked with his son Ben to make a model of the solar system. They found that if you're going to make a model that's true to the size of the planets in the solar system and the distance between the planets, that model is going to have to be mighty big.

In terms of scale, the Van Dusens' solar system is tiny. "The planets are one-billionth the actual size, and the distance between them is one-billionth the actual distance." You can see from the picture how big the sun is (behind Jack). "Earth is about a half inch in diameter," says Jack.

Ben was in fourth grade when he and his father painted the solar system on the bike path near their house. "It was $20 worth of paint, but lots of excitement. People would ask, 'What are you guys doing?' Everybody just loved it. But the city came out and stripped the sun off the sidewalk, because somebody thought it might be too slippery. We decided to try to do something that could be more permanent."

The answer was steel planets and a sun, costing some $12,000, which Jack raised through grants and donations. The sun is located in the middle of Alton Baker

Park, along the Willamette River in Eugene. "We wanted it to be somewhere that families could come, see the sun, then just bike on out to Pluto, 3.7 miles away."

Next, the Van Dusens considered adding the nearest star. "We weren't sure how far away it would be," says Jack. "Brazil, maybe?" But it turned out that to represent the distance from the sun to the nearest star, you'd have to place a model star 95 percent of the way around the world—which is almost back where you started. "The nearest star would be close to Oklahoma City," says Jack. "We were afraid people might think it was closer than it really is."

Jack and Ben show off the steel models of the planets with the sun for the only time before they were spread around the model solar system.

Neptune's moon 4,429,508,700 miles away, thrilled Earthlings. Now the Grand Tour is known as the Voyager Interstellar Mission. It's still winging away from Earth at 290 million miles a year.

Pluto hasn't been explored, but a mission is planned to the faraway planet, its moon, Charon, and the Kuiper belt of asteroids and comets beyond Pluto. The

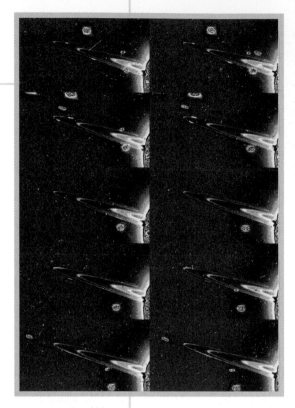

Five pairs of Hubble Space Telescope images work together to give a view of the orbit of Saturn's moons. Like stereoscopes (see Chapter 4), these pairs give a fuller view than just one alone would.

What else can the Hubble Space Telescope do? Take pictures with the NICMOS (Near Infrared Camera and Multi-Object Spectrometer). This instrument captures Saturn's infrared light, which helps map what's in Saturn's atmosphere.

Pluto-Kuiper Express is expected to launch in 2012.

The latest plan? Balloons that can rise into the atmosphere as balloons have since the 1700s (they are the oldest way of flying for people), but with some differences. These ULDBs (Ultra Long Duration Balloons) can stay up longer. When they're done with their missions, a radio command can tell them to drop back down to Earth.

These balloons can be used to study outer space. They float telescopes that are too big for a rocket to carry high into orbit. But they may also be used in a different way. Other planets have atmospheres, too, and scientists hope they can put balloons into orbit on those planets to study them and their atmospheres. They've already tried it by sending two balloons to Venus—with success.

What We Can See

In 1863, Friedrich Argelander published the Bonn Survey, which featured 324,189 stars in the Northern Hemisphere alone. He added parts of the Southern Hemisphere to it in 1886, and a team of astronomers from Argentina added the rest by 1908. Stars above the South Pole were added by 1930. And astronomers have been adding more and more stars to the picture ever since.

Getting a clear picture of the universe hasn't been easy. For one thing, seeing isn't really believing. The light that we see coming from other stars started its journey so long ago that by now the stars might actually have burned out. Certainly many of them are different at this precise moment from the way they look to us. These days many astronomers think it's hardly worth charting stars, because there

Andromeda, our nearest galaxy, is just 2.9 million light-years away.

are billions of galaxies out in space, each with hundreds of billions of stars.

Is it possible to picture a universe so large? Sure, say astronomers and map-makers. If it's possible to map something as microscopic as a cell (see Chapter 7), then why not something as enormous as a universe?

Galaxies are incredibly far away, so far away they need their own system of measurement. Near ones are measured in parsecs. A parsec is 3.26 light-years. Farther ones are measured in kiloparsecs (1,000 parsecs = 3,260 light-years) or megaparsecs (1,000 kiloparsecs, or 3,260,000 light-years). There are longer measurements than that: feintoseconds, picograms, nanoseconds . . . Far out? You bet.

Listening to the Stars

Until the 20th century, the stars people charted were those that could be seen with the naked eye or with telescopes that picked up the starlight and magnified it so that it could be seen with the naked eye. But in 1930, telephone company researchers trying to get rid of static on international phone lines realized that part of what they were hearing was something nobody had ever thought of: star noise. After all, most light waves are invisible. Astronomers realized that what they needed to do to find more stars was to come up with instruments that could

MY MAP AND ME

Jocelyn Bell Burnell

This array of radio antennas helped Jocelyn Bell Burnell discover something she called Little Green Men. What else could be creating those flashes of light?

Jocelyn Bell Burnell helped discover pulsars, very heavy neutron stars that spin. She continued studying radio astronomy, exploring stars and light waves across the spectrum, from gamma rays to infrared rays. She talked to me about her experiences eavesdropping on the stars.

Q. Why is it important for people to know what's in the universe and where it is—to have a map of the universe?

A. We are, literally, made of star stuff—the carbon, oxygen, calcium, and so on in our bodies came from previous generations of stars which died and then their material was recycled. So we have a very intimate connection with the universe. People also seem to want to know where we are in the scheme of things—that we inhabit a planet orbiting a very ordinary star, with an inconspicuous place in a typical galaxy, etc.

Q. How did the discovery of pulsars affect the mapping of the universe?

A. The discovery of pulsars has not yet affected the mapping of the universe. When the era of interstellar travel comes, pulsars could well be used as navigation beacons—lighthouses—in space. They are also useful to the astronomer who is interested in knowing in detail how our galaxy rotates.

Q. When you realized you'd found something new in the universe, was the experience comparable to an earth-explorer discovering a new ocean or continent? What does it feel like to be on the edge of Terra Incognita?

A. In olden days, the explorers saw the new landfall with their eyes. Radio astronomers are working via the medium of radio waves and radio telescopes and are several stages removed from seeing things directly with their eyes. So when they "see" something unusual, they have a lot of extra work to do convincing themselves that the thing is real and not an artifact [a quirk] of their equipment. This draws out the discovery process. All research, in whatever field, is by definition on the edge of Terra Cognita, and its purpose is to extend Terra Cognita into Terra Incognita. You have to be comfortable with change if you are a research scientist!

pick up wavelengths of light that were outside the narrow visible range. Star noise was the beginning of *radio astronomy*.

Grote Reber, an Illinois astronomer, was among the first people to put up a radio dish antenna in their yards. In 1940, he announced that he'd found a hissing sound that came from the Milky Way itself. By 1944, Reber published the first radio map of the Milky Way, showing all the places sound came from—places where stars were. Radio astronomy helped put stars on the map that couldn't be seen with a telescope.

After that, things got even more technical. During the 1950s and 1960s, scientists figured out how to identify molecules of hydrogen, ammonia, water, and carbon monoxide, and through this, how to find the places where stars were being "born." Astronomers had long known that the nebulae—such as Horsehead Nebula, Crab Nebula, and Orion Nebula in the Milky Way—were places where stars were forming. But molecular astronomy allowed them to explore right through the hearts of the nebulae and to number their newborn stars. One of their findings: The nebulae were tens of thousands of light-years from one side to the other, with the mass of 1,000 suns.

What am I seeing? A map laid over a photograph of the winter sky shows some constellations.

Today's star atlases are made with spectral mapping, capturing light waves from all areas of the spectrum. In the 1970s, a tool called the CCD (*charge-coupled device*) used silicon chips that fired a pulse when they were hit by light. CCDs let astronomers begin large-scale surveys of the sky.

A CCD picture looks like a photograph, but really isn't. Add this information to that picked

A star is born! A CCD captures light waves from a faraway nebula, where novae—forming stars—create flows of energy that look like clouds.

up by the huge (10 meters across) twin Keck telescopes in Hawaii; the Hubble Telescope orbiting 370 miles above Earth; a mammoth radio telescope in Arecibo, Puerto Rico; infrared and microwave detectors from satellites; balloons floating in the atmosphere with their instruments aimed toward outer space; the new VLT (Very Large Telescope) that will be stronger than the Hubble . . . Wow! The total picture of space is incredibly vast. Trying to map it means taking a tiny slice and analyzing it deeply. Each time someone does it, incredible surprises pop up.

MAPMAKER

John Briggs

John Briggs is a telescope engineer at the University of Chicago's Yerkes Observatory. He is helping to survey and map the biggest piece of the universe ever. The Sloan Digital Sky Survey will map in detail one-quarter of the entire sky, determining the positions and brightnesses of more than 100 million celestial objects. Astronomers and engineers will use two telescopes at Apache Point, New Mexico, to measure the distances to more than a million galaxies and quasars. One purpose is to see the distribution of galactic sheets (places with lots of stars) and voids (places without stars) in the universe. This will help scientists understand how the universe was formed and how it has developed and changed.

"In a lot of ways the Sloan Survey is like a road map for giant telescopes (like the Keck telescopes in Hawaii). Our bigger telescope is really not so giant—2.5 meters in diameter—100 inches. A camera attached to the telescope lets us see clearly across a wide field of view, and it measures the positions, brightness, and color of objects very accurately." The Sloan Survey uses its smaller telescope—just 0.5 meter, or 20 inches, in diameter—to give special attention to about a million especially interesting-looking objects found in its chunk of sky.

"We've chosen this part of the sky to map because we are actually looking away from the Milky Way, away from the light of the stars in our own huge galaxy." In April 2000, the Sloane Survey pointed the way to a quasar located a record-breaking 14 billion light-years away. Finding new farthest-away objects gives scientists a new number for the size and age of the universe. By the time this book is published, the record may already have been broken.

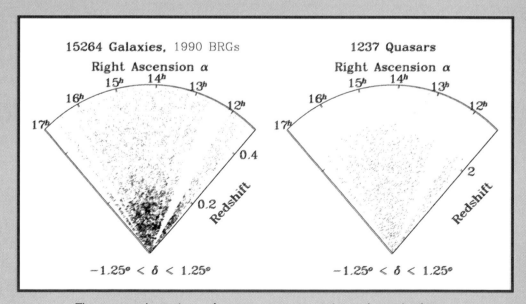

The star search continues. Astronomers are surveying and mapping larger and larger portions of the sky. This map from the Sloan Digital Sky Survey shows a slice of the sky where three million galaxies were found.

The Map of the Universe

Cosmologists are like doctors studying a person. The galaxies are like cells, there are so many of them. And mapping a piece of the cosmos is like taking a blood sample: You can guess that what you find in one area is pretty much true of another.

A famous piece of the cosmos is the one John Huchra and Margaret J. Geller plotted in the Northern Hemisphere. If you look into the night sky, you can find their piece close to the Big Dipper, in the constellation Coma Berenices. The two cosmologists found a "Great Wall" of galaxies, the largest *thing* that humans have ever seen. Their map revealed 1,074 galaxies in an area 500 million light-years long. That's 5,000 times the size of the Milky Way. The Milky Way has 100 billion stars. You do the math.

Down south, astronomers at Las Campanas, Chile, surveyed a slice of space stretching across one to two billion light-years. Their result was six maps that showed the positions of more than 26,000 galaxies. That's a lot of Great Walls.

Even larger celestial surveys are already underway, including an English-Australian one meant to map 250,000 galaxies, and an American-Japanese project to find the distance from Earth to one million galaxies over half the sky—20 times more than the Las Campanas survey.

And then there is the Sloan Digital Sky Survey, which aims to map a quarter of the sky, the largest chunk ever. (See page 102.) Where will it end? Maybe *Toy Story*'s Buzz Lightyear has the best answer: "To infinity and beyond!"

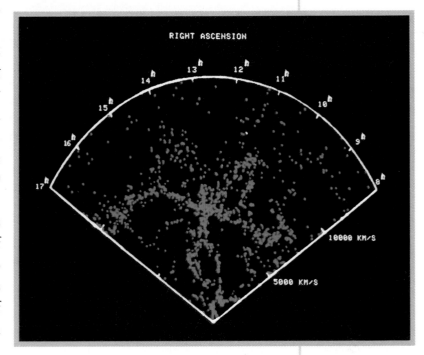

RIGHT ASCENSION

10000 KM/S

5000 KM/S

A redshift survey of part of the north celestial hemisphere showed a "Great Wall" of stars millions of light-years long.

CHAPTER 7

Beyond Geography

How do you hold a place in your mind? Picture a place that's very close to home—your mouth. Can you imagine the part of your mouth from which you lost your last tooth? Now picture the Milky Way, a big pancake shot through with stars. Picture the clear bubble of a cell of onion skin. Picture a place in a book, even if you've never been there, even if it's a place the author made up. Picture a car, a candy bar, the Internet.

How can all these different-size places fit into the "picture" part of your brain? How can maps of these places fit onto one page of this book? How can there be so many maps?

This chapter can't begin to contain the thousands of new maps being created as the 21st century begins. Mapping started out as a way to help people get from one geographical place to another. Now mapping has gone far beyond geography. Maps now show places that are "off the map," out of this world, deep inside it, huge, tiny, or not findable in any physical place at all. Maps don't stand still anymore; they change at the push of a computer button. Every new piece of information can create a new map. Maps can diagram action or show it like a movie. They show connections that nobody ever sees, inside computers or inside the brain. They show imaginary rivers such as the path a coin takes from hand to hand or the path of handshakes from one person to the next. And they show ideas that don't have any physical basis at all.

For the future, two rules that seem opposites hold sway over cartography:
1. If you can picture something in your mind, even if there's no real data, you can make a map of it.
2. If you can gather data about something, even if you can't imagine what it is, you can make a map of it.

Where the Brain Goes

Having an image of a place is so important to human beings.

Say you and your dog were dropped into some unknown place in the wild. Which of you would find food first? Which of you would find the way home? Your dog is naturally set up to sniff out food. Like animals, we can follow our noses or use a sense of direction that, scientists say, might have to do with light or Earth's

MAPMAKER

David Gold

Every new LEGO set comes with visual directions that are a map for action. They also show what pieces to use and how to put them together. Showing every step is important for a toy that is used in many different countries. You don't need to read to build from LEGO's directions.

David Gold creates the directions. If you think this is a simple job, consider this: "You start with the model in front of you," Gold says. "You draw the instructions backwards."

LEGO designers use the computer program 3D Autocad to draw their instructions. "You break up the thing on your desk," says Gold. The Autocad program already has standard LEGO pieces programmed into it. Gold selects the right pieces to build the model on the computer screen. "Once you've got the whole thing on the screen, you unbuild it, pulling off pieces from the top. The first pieces you take off become the last pieces

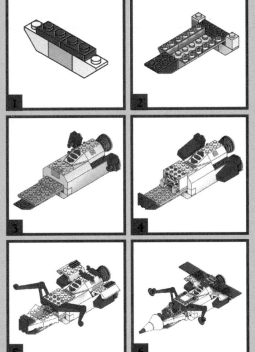

The LEGO* diagram shows you how to do something. First it shows, then you act.

the builder will put on." He takes the model apart layer by layer, trying to create logical steps—but backward!—for someone building from scratch.

When he's done, Gold follows his steps in forward order, checking to see if the model can really be built from the bottom up, according to his steps. "Someone else may test it, too—other adults or kids. If I can build it then a lot of kids can."

Gold himself was the kind of kid who could build anything from a LEGO set without instructions. "My parents say I was always good at putting things together." When Gold grew up, he became an architect, which involves creating blueprints, detailed maps of a building that show not just what is there, but how to build it. Blueprints are an example of mapping something that isn't yet there—and mapping out actions to take to create it.

magnetism. But humans do something that no animal has ever done: plan a route based on understanding of what's between *here* and *there*. We're naturally set up to figure out where we are, to determine which way is home, and to plan a way to get there. Just as animals migrate one step or sniff at a time, humans seem to have an instinct for making places into images—in our minds or in our hands. Those images are maps.

Part of this natural mapping ability lies in recognizing and remembering shapes. Americans recognize the shape of the United States, whether it's upside down, right side up, blown up, shrunk down, or backward. The shape of a place is like notes our brains take to help us remember it.

Another part of this natural ability lies in navigating through our image of a place—getting around or making connections between one place and another by using mental maps. Scientists studying the brain have been able to pinpoint which part of the brain becomes active when maps are used or imagined. Studies of London taxi drivers, who are required to know their city by heart, found that the map-remembering part of the average driver's brain—the hippocampus—was larger than that of someone who didn't need to have as many mental maps on file. What's more, says National Science Foundation scientist Lawrence Parsons, the hippocampus is one of the "oldest" parts of the brain. While other areas—such as the writing area, for instance, or the memory center for remembering phone numbers—have grown or developed over the course of human history—the hippocampus has been there since early humans walked the earth. People have always mapped—in their heads, first, and in other ways, later.

Maps on the Brain

The process by which the brain puts together an image of a place is a lot like the way cartographers make maps. First, it establishes the basic shape. Then it adds details, routes, landmarks, and other information about the place. Consider the difference between a city you know only in maps and a city you've visited in person. How is your memory different? How is your understanding of the map different?

Maps help us make sense of the confusion of information around us. They take a huge pile of pictures and images and make one basic image that unites them and makes them simpler.

Here's how it works. The retina is a little mirror in your eye. When you see something, the retina reflects it exactly, then sends the image point by point to your brain. The brain interprets it, and turns it into something you can use. That's how you can use a two-dimensional map to get around in a three-dimensional world. It's also how you can take a three-dimensional place and turn it into a two-dimensional map.

CalTech scientist John Allman found that the map-remembering part of the brain actually forms structures that are like maps. Form enough of them, and your hippocampus expands, like the London taxi drivers'.

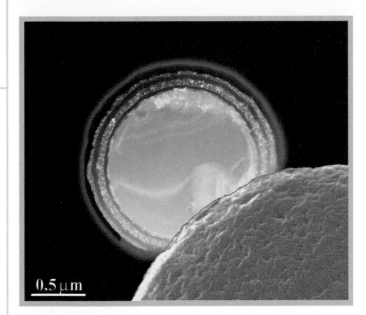

Earth and the moon? No. This is a cross section of a tiny particle of iron, looked at through an ultrathin film. The stripes at the edge of the blue piece show the layers in the iron.

What do the electrons in the cells of a ceramic material look like close-up? A transmission electron microscope mapped them.

The Eye of the Mind

Galileo realized that Jupiter's moons were just a few of the things a telescope could see, and he recognized that as technology improved, many more things that were invisible so far would suddenly pop into view. A few years back the biggest thing ever mapped was the Great Wall of galaxies 500 million light-years long (see Chapter 6). By the time this book is published, something bigger may have been mapped.

So what's the smallest thing ever mapped? Cells? Not even close. Molecules? Nope. Atoms? Not quite. In the late 1940s, particle accelerators came into widespread use. These machines smashed atoms, splitting them into protons, neutrons, and electrons. Microscopes even let physicists map the outlines of electrons.

By making atom smashers longer and longer, physicists smashed atoms into smaller smithereens. In the early 1970s, atom smashers between two and four miles long revealed the existence of quarks, which make up the nucleus of an atom.

Physicists hope that the superconducting supercollider will smash atoms into even smaller particles. This machine, which hasn't been built yet, would use a 54-mile atom-smashing track. It might simulate the conditions of the Big Bang—and prove the existence of *dark matter*, tiny particles that might make up most of the mass of the universe. Once the supercollider is built, maps of dark matter may be big news.

While cells are not the smallest things ever mapped, they are among the most important. Cells are the basic structure of living things—like bricks in a building.

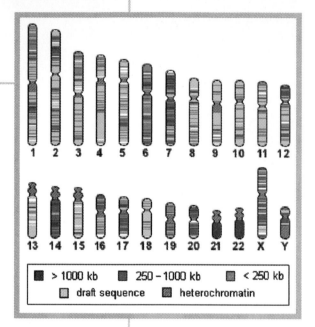

Mapping the human genome meant figuring out what order every tiny piece came in.

> > 1000 kb   250 – 1000 kb   < 250 kb
> draft sequence   heterochromatin

There are 100 trillion cells in each person's body. (Imagine that; now imagine 100 trillion stars in the universe. They're all there—and you couldn't count them in a lifetime of counting!) Every cell has 3 billion DNA (dioxyribonucleic acids). Scientists map the structure of DNA by figuring out which acid fits where. How each cell's DNA fits together determines what kind of cell it is. By mapping it, scientists can copy it, change it, and understand it. In the future, this could mean cures for diseases, prevention of birth defects, and cloning—making exact genetic copies of living things.

Slice and Dice

Just as exciting as getting down to the size of electrons or out to the edge of the universe is getting deep inside something to see it in new ways. Sometimes the best way to understand how something is made—like an airliner, a bone, or a thunderstorm—is to slice it in half and look inside. You wouldn't want to do that with a person, a jet, or a building. But maps can do it for us.

Cross sections are slices through an object. You don't really cut it. You draw it as though it had been cut, using the information you have about it. A cross section of the *Titanic*, for example, would show all the different decks. By looking at it, you could get a good idea of how the ship worked—and why it sank.

A CT scan shows a cross section of the human body. The back is at the top.

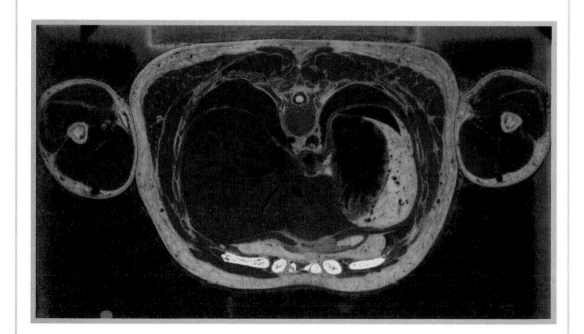

MY MAP AND ME
Lillian Jeng

Lillian Jeng is studying for her doctoral degree in geography at Syracuse University. I pictured her sitting with a pen and paper drawing maps. Boy, was I wrong! Instead of drawing maps, Jeng is learning how to use them to help beat diseases. Her field is called *medical geography.*

"I was planning to go into the Peace Corps [a volunteer organization that helps people in developing countries] when I found out that my dad had Lou Gehrig's disease. I didn't want to be far away, so I rearranged my plans. Then, after reading about my dad's illness (doctors still don't know how people get it), it seemed that there might be geographical components (parts) to it that weren't being studied properly."

Jeng wanted to look closer at Lou Gehrig's disease—and others—to find out whether it happened more frequently in certain places, and whether the disease could be related to factors in the environment. Medical geography involves making maps that show this information.

Remember Dr. John Snow, the London doctor who linked a list of cholera cases (cholera is an infection passed through water) to maps that showed public pumps? (See Chapter 1.) By doing this, he figured out which pump was spreading the disease. His map was an early example of medical geography.

Maps are only as good as the information they're made from. "Let's say you're trying to find out whether people have higher rates of a disease in one place than another by showing rates by county. But are the rates accurate?" Jeng says that some areas are less likely to report occurrences of certain illnesses—food poisoning, for one—because the reports from some doctors or clinics are different from others. If everyone doesn't report things in the same way, then you don't get accurate information—or an accurate map. "My main goal as a medical geographer is to find ways to improve the way we collect health data, particularly data relating to things people are exposed to in the environment and illnesses they get from that." Could mapping be the key to better medical care? Yes, says Jeng.

Imagine that someone cut six candy bars in half and asked you to identify them. To get an idea of what this might be like, check out the candy bar cross sections on the Web site of San Francisco's Exploratorium, www.exploratorium.com. A CT ("cat") scan is a kind of mapmaking machine used in medicine to get a cross section of part of the body. When you have a CT scan, you lie down in a machine that's like a body-sized tunnel. Light rays fire at you from all sides. The result is a map slice that shows things in their correct positions and shapes—different from a flat X ray that shows what your 3-D body is like.

Cutaways can show processes that happen "behind closed doors"—or just behind walls. The cutaway view of the New York Public Library on page 110 shows how books from the seven-story-high tower of bookshelves reach the reference room on the top floor. Library patrons fill out a request slip. The slips pass through pneumatic tubes like big vacuum cleaner hoses. Library workers fill the requests. The books are sucked back up to the reference room and placed in the patrons' hands. (For more cutaways, see the map of the earth's core on page 85.)

The New York Public Library has seven stories of stacks of books. If you want a book, a librarian goes to get it. You don't get to go into the stacks. This cutaway view shows patrons what they never get to see.

What Diagrams Show

Cross sections, cutaways, and see-through views are three examples of diagrams. More than just drawings, diagrams show how things work. They can also tell you how to do things, and they can demonstrate how things are done. An explosion is another kind of diagram that was drawn with the user in mind. It takes parts that fit close together in a machine or body and moves them apart. This lets the viewer see each part on its own, separate from the others, and also to see more clearly how the parts fit together to make the machine work.

MAPS MAKE THE DIFFERENCE

Jessica K. Hodgins

Video games often feature real-life athletes and movie stars that move in a way you can recognize. But how do you copy a real person's movements—and imitate or adapt them for the screen?

Jessica K. Hodgins, an animator and scientist at the Georgia Institute of Technology, explains. Movement mappers attach markers to the body of an athlete and have him or her go through the motions of the sport. In the case of an athlete like Tiger Woods, who posed for a California video game maker, Electronic Arts, that meant swinging different golf clubs, walking, picking up his ball out of the cup, and so on. For Tiger Woods's video game, the markers correspond to places on a special "Tiger" grid on the computer, which was made based on pictures and movies of him. The animators use that data to make the

Sensors helped make a map of Tiger Woods' golf swing for a video game.

Woods told Golf Digest *that he was looking forward to playing virtual golf matches against himself.*

movements of the video game cartoon Tiger match the real Tiger's ways of moving.

In video games and other applications that let the user interact with characters, animators have to map the motion based on what is happening in the *virtual* world of the game. Say the video game features tennis. "Eventually we have a library of tennis motions," says Hodgins. This remapping of the recorded motion would allow a character in an animation to be able to handle tennis balls that come in from the left, the right, high, and low, and fast and slow as well.

Hodgins hopes to use what she has learned to control humanoid robots.

But how does that machine work? Can a map be used to show movement, action, and interaction? Yes—through diagrams. Diagrams are maps of things, places, or situations. Like maps of land, they show the connections between points. On a land map, this map may be land or water. On a diagram, it may be action. A diagram may show us one step or part or many. It's designed to help us understand something. It's designed to help us do something.

A computer flowchart shows the process a person goes through when using a computer program. The computer user may make choices, and the arrows on the flowchart point to what comes next as the result of each choice.

Manhattan Bus Map
January 2000

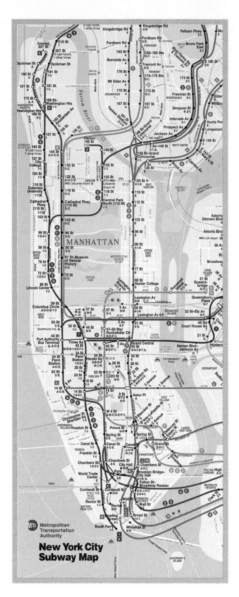

New York City Subway Map

What does a bus map show about a place (left) . . . and why does a subway map show something different? (right)

A tent diagram sheet shows how to put up your own tent. It breaks down the process into visual steps to follow. If you understand the concept of steps, then you can follow this diagram to pitch the tent—no matter how old you are, whether you can read, or what language you speak.

A diagram can also show you how a movement works. The action happens, and the diagram tells you how.

Point by point, scientists can precisely map a physical movement and use it to play copycat. At first, this technology went to work to help athletes or dancers figure out the best way to do a movement. Now doctors can map body parts, trace blood flow, and follow patterns of pain or disease.

Animators can even put together all a person's movements with a model of the person's face or body to make virtual people. At the Rock and Roll Hall of Fame in Seattle, Washington, computer artists and animators are working to make a copycat James Brown who dances and sings exactly like the original. What does he sing? "I Feel Good!" (For more, see page 111.)

Piano music is a map of the keyboard, a diagram that dictates action. The staff (the lines) stands for the places where the notes are on the keyboard. The notes themselves show you what action to take, when, and how. Computer keyboarding teacher Elspeth Sladden designed a map to help students learn which fingers to use for which keys. You might think that the map of a piano keyboard and the map of a computer keyboard wouldn't be very different. But in one, different fingers play different notes. In the other, the same keys are always hit by the same fingers. The action a diagram demonstrates has a lot to do with how the diagram is best drawn.

Compare the two maps of New York City. One shows bus lines; one shows the New York City subway. The subway map, like many train maps, shows train lines that are not in their real geographical positions. It's mapped the way it's used. When you transfer from one line to another, you don't need to know where the lines cross *in the city*, because you're not getting out there, just changing directions toward your destination. The subway map is drawn in a way that makes it most clear how to reach your destination. It's not meant to represent the physical layout of the stations as they really are in the city, but as you use them.

Out of Their Minds: Maps From Fantasy

A map is a way of showing graphically—even if not *geographically*—whatever is in that mapping part of your mind. What this means is that you can make a map of something that you haven't experienced in real life. Even if it isn't a place you can go to physically, you can still go there by mapping it. To understand this, consider places in books. Have you ever been to the Hundred Acre Wood (from *Winnie-the-Pooh*), Narnia (*The Lion, the Witch, and the Wardrobe*), Florin (*The Princess Bride*), or Middle Earth (*The Hobbit*)?

If you can describe a place detail by detail, you can map it. The imagination of writers and artists makes invented places real. Stories trace the path of heroes through these fantasy places. Fantasy writer Orson Scott Card often starts his stories not by writing, but by mapping his setting.

This see-through view of a Volkswagen Beetle maps out the Bug's guts in a way nobody—even car factory workers—ever gets to see.

MAPMAKER

Patrice Ivan

Patrice Ivan read *The Island of the Blue Dolphins* for a class she was taking to become a teacher, and saw a map in its pages. "*The Island of the Blue Dolphins* is about a Native American girl on an island. The island is described so well that I began to visualize it. I kept seeing its shape—the dolphin shape—come alive. I found more than 50 references in the book to where things were, directional indicators, and more. Karenna, the girl in the book, was all alone. I wanted to show how she moved throughout the island and why she changed locations, fishing areas, living areas. I developed a key for the relief stuff, the places where there were hills or cliffs. And the story came alive for me, in three-dimensional form in my mind—and then in two-dimensional form in my map. Maybe if someone else imagined that island, their map would come out a different way."

In computer games, you get to be the story's hero yourself, navigating along through real or imagined landscapes like the Amazon River, the moon, or the island of Myst. Other computer programs allow you to make the place yourself—either by adding a city to land or creating the land yourself. Through virtual reality, we cross the line between real life and our imaginings. To mapmakers, the line doesn't matter much anymore. The fact that we can map things outside our experience gives us a door to new worlds—the parts of our universe that can only be guessed at, the insides of genes, the tiny cells that make us who we are.

A Map of Me

Imagine drawing a map of your own body. What do you like most about yourself? What hurts? Where are your scars, your strengths, your weaknesses?

The Renaissance in Europe—from the 1400s to the 1600s—was a rich time for geographical maps of faraway places. Oddly enough, while some mapmakers were exploring the edges of the earth, others felt that they already knew the world as well as the backs of their hands. These mapmakers used the hand as a symbol of the place where the real world met the imaginary world. They realized that touching something with your hand created a map in the brain, so that the next time you came to that thing, you could identify it. In a sense, you'd know where you were. Hands could be used as windows to your inner self—or as tools to help you understand the world outside yourself.

Have you ever had your palm "read"? People who believe in palmistry believe that your hand holds clues to your past, present, and future—and that it can be read like a map. Others believe that your entire body is a map to the universe as it relates to you. Different parts of you are said to be ruled by changes in different parts of the sky—and maps exist that show this. A map of the foot is sometimes used to help treat ailments. The spots in the foot where the nerves end are linked to the parts of the body served by those nerves—and if there's a problem there, it can be dealt with in part by treating the key part of the foot.

Are these things a matter of belief or science? Some people live by them—and others don't. Of course all the parts of the body are connected. And of course people are connected to the universe. But can you really map such connections?

Hold That Thought!

What about ideas? Can you map the path your ideas take from one thought to another? Can you see the connections? When I was growing up, I wasn't often asked to map my thoughts. But kids today are.

Venn diagrams are a simple way of mapping ideas and the connections between them. What do the Mets have in common with the Yankees? What's different about the two teams? As you can see, Venn diagrams work for both facts and opinions.

You can also make semantic maps as a way of linking ideas for something you're thinking about or analyzing or planning. The map I drew of the map stuff I found while I was working on this book has categories. Another kind of map might show how I went from one idea to another, like following a path in my mind.

Yes, the Mets and Yanks do have things in common. They're in the intersection of this Venn diagram.

Mets circle: play in Shea Stadium / from Queens / won two World Series / really great!

Intersection: wear blue / play in New York / play baseball

Yankees circle: play in Yankee Stadium / from the Bronx / won a lot of World Series / really stink!

Mets   Yankees

Where should I put the map game I just found? Which group? What else could be in that group?

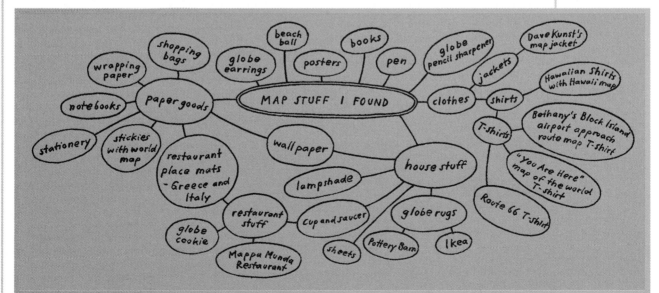

MAPMAKER

Lawrence M. Parsons

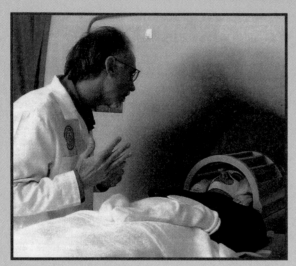

Laurence M. Parsons asks a patient to think about something specific. A PET scan will help map the path the thought takes through the patient's brain.

Dr. Lawrence M. Parsons, who works at the National Science Foundation in Arlington, Virginia, is one of a worldwide network of scientists working to create an atlas of the brain.

Q. Why do we need brain maps?

A. By comparing lots of people as they do the same kind of task, we begin to draw conclusions about parts of the brain that do the same kind of work in every person. We're maybe a hundred years away from having a real atlas of the brain. But now surgeons who face removing tumors or doing other kinds of brain surgery have some help figuring out which parts of the brain are most crucial to a person.

Q. How do you map a thought?

A. What we'll do is ask a person to do a certain kind of thinking: read a sentence, think about picking up a glass, remember a piece of information. We use MRIs (magnetic resonance imaging) and PET (position emission tomography) scans to monitor the flow of blood through the brain. Five or six seconds after a part of the brain has been active, fresh blood flows there. There's a little delay, but we can follow and chase the fresh blood through the brain and find a path used when the person does a certain kind of thinking task. The brain is like a Swiss Army knife, with lots of little parts that each do a specific kind of work. When something happens in the brain, lots of those little parts work together to make it happen. We're using new technology to eavesdrop on how things happen in the brain.

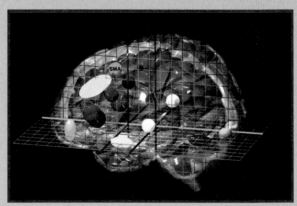

This map, made from many PET scans, shows the parts of the brain used to solve a specific problem. The yellow areas are involved in choosing words. The red are parts related to speaking movements. The blue are parts that allow us to read. The orange are parts that relate to hearing our own voices when we speak. The green are parts that give us short-term memory for word meaning.

In a brand-new kind of mapping, scientists have turned their brains inside out to make maps, following a movement that's extremely close to home: thoughts. How can you map thoughts? For a clue, consider something much farther away: stars. In the early days of astronomy, humans looked up and saw the stars. Even way back then, it wasn't enough for them to name individual stars. No, they saw groups of stars as pictures, and their maps showed connections between the stars. It was a way of trying to understand what the heavens meant to Earth. Later on, celestial maps included new constellations, and contained long catalogs of stars. Astronomers today still study individual stars, but they recognize that what's *between* the stars may hold as many clues to the universe as the stars themselves.

At first, neurology—the study of the brain—focused on mapping the brain by finding out what parts of the brain hold what information. Figuring out that the hippocampus holds maps is one example of this. Neurologists have determined where long-term memory, such as what happened in kindergarten, and short-term memory, such as today's schedule, are stored. But new technology is letting neurologists trace the route of a thought through the brain.

Here's how it works. A PET (position emission tomography) scan forms the basic map of the brain for the person being studied. Next, the person does a task: solves a problem or answers a question that requires a certain kind of brain function. The person might be asked to spell a word or identify a photograph. Special instruments help the scientists see which parts of the brain "light up" while the person does the task.

A supercomputer connects those lit-up parts with the same parts on the PET scan, and the person's thought process appears on that map in a matter of minutes, a movie of a thought as it crosses the brain.

Did you know the Internet had a backbone, something like our spine, which sends messages from the brain to the rest of the body? The Internet's backbone—the Mbone—is mapped here.

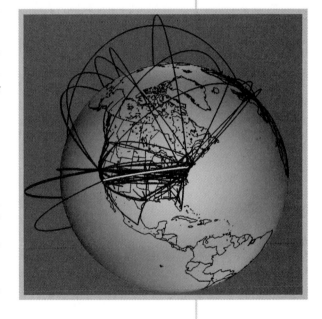

Invisible Rivers

If you can think about thoughts and map them, can you map places that you only visit by computer? Think of what you imagine when you click a link to go to a new Web site on the Internet. How is it possible to "go" to another place while your physical body still sits in your chair? In mapping the Internet, cartographers put physical parameters on a place that only exists in the imagination. Compare the maps on this page and the next. What kind of information do you get from them? How do they help you understand what happens on the Internet? Can you think of a better way to map Internet connections? Does the Internet *need* to be mapped?

You don't need a map of the Internet to get around. Internet mappers have another reason for their art. Just as getting a bird's-eye view of land changed the way people saw things, getting a view of the way people connect through their computers will help our understanding of how the Web works. What are the different routes people take to get to your site? Why does one site get more hits than another? Maps may provide the answers.

MAPMAKER

Bill Cheswick

"The idea behind mapping the Internet is to see who's connected to whom," says Bill Cheswick, who created this map for Lucent Technologies, part of Bell Laboratories.

The process, Cheswick says, was simple enough. "You put data into the computer, and 20 hours of computer time later, the map comes out."

The map was created to let Cheswick's company, Lucent Technologies, see where their information packets went. "There are 140,000 people, and our network connects to 40 countries. Trying to figure out what information went from data listing the connections was impossible, out of control! But the map shows us how it works."

Why would they want to know? One reason is for basic information, but the other is troubleshooting. Cheswick is often involved in decisions about how the Internet can be protected. Is it under attack? Yes, in the sense that people don't always get the information they need. The attacks may be simple, such as electricity shutting down in areas where there are earthquakes, floods, or even wars.

Cheswick has also been involved in helping prevent attacks from computer attackers who would like to bring down the Internet. The U.S. government, too, wants to protect the Net in case of war. "In 1996, we got together to discuss what problems the United States might have in 2005," says Cheswick.

As with other mapped actions, the pattern in the map was something of a surprise. "There are spokes and hubs [like bicycle wheels] on the Internet map. Those are places where lots of information goes in and out. You can't see that in tables of connections." But a map shows the pattern, and the eye picks up on it immediately. "The human eye is a wonderful organ for finding problems quickly, and in understanding situations," says Cheswick. "It's like Magellan being able to look at a satellite picture of the Pacific, seeing an island and saying, 'Let's go check that out.' The map makes it possible to see what might be worth a closer look."

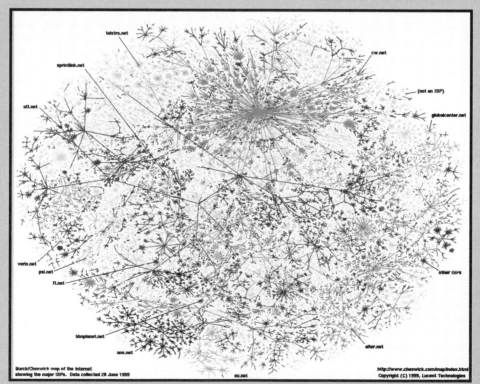

How do you map Internet connections? Here's another way.

People are interested in mapping many other kinds of invisible connections. Have you taken part in a teddy bear project? Classes send a teddy bear on a trip with a friend. The friend's job is to pass the bear to another traveler. The bear carries a "passport" in which the travelers record their names, journeys, and the places where they pass the bear on. It's fun—and surprising—to see just how far one small bear can go in a short time. It's interesting to see the connections between people—who knows whom—and how the bear gets back home.

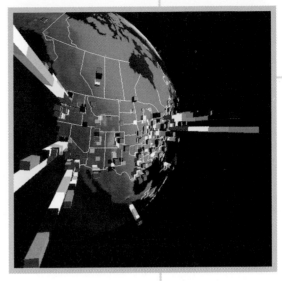

Where are the country's Internet hot spots?

Who knows whom is exactly the subject of another game, called Six Degrees of Kevin Bacon. The game starts by naming an actor, and the challenge is to link that person with the actor Kevin Bacon. Links would be movies that people worked on. Say the other actor was Eddie Murphy. Here's an example of the links: Eddie Murphy is person 1. He worked with person 2 on one movie, person 2 worked with person 3 on another movie, person 3 with person 4, person 4 with person 5, and person 5 with Kevin Bacon. If you can connect the two actors in six links—or six degrees of separation— then you win. Who knows who—or who has worked with who—is another kind of invisible river. You don't have to be famous, either. Other mappers have explored the possibilities of this idea, which is sometimes called the "small world" theory. A west coast scientist did an experiment to see how many links it would take to send a package from the west coast to a certain person on the east coast without using an address. Passers had to think of someone they knew who might know the person in question—or who might know someone who knew the person—and send it along. Most of the time it took less than six links.

Do you know where this bear has been? There's no place that can't be mapped.

If you could follow a drop of water from the mountains down a river to the sea and around the world's oceans, you could draw a map of an incredible journey. Money passes along another invisible river, as does air. You're breathing air that could have been breathed already by anyone else in the world—past or present. It could have been breathed by the first cave person who drew a map in the dirt. And wouldn't he or she have been amazed by the maps in your lap?

Maps expand the world. They stretch your mind. They give you new worlds to wander through in your imagination. Armchair traveler? With a map you can go anywhere. It isn't such a small world after all, is it?

Books

Younger:

The Amazing Pop-Up Geography Book by Kate Pelty (Dutton, 2000)

Atlas in the Round by Keith Lye and Alastair Campbell (Running Press, 1999)

Barron's Geography Wizard for Kids by Margaret Kenda and Phyllis A. Williams (Barron's Educational Services, 1997)

Barron's Great Explorers series, for example: *Captain Cook and His Exploration of the Pacific* by Roger Morriss (Barron's Educational Series, 1998)

The Book of Where or How to Be Naturally Geographic by Neill Bell (Little Brown, 1982)

Discovery of the Americas (prehistory-Columbus) by Betsy and Giulio Maestro (Mulberry, 1991)

Earthsearch: A Kids' Geography Museum in a Book by John Cassidy (Klutz Press, 1994)

Exploration and Conquest (the Americas after Columbus 1500–1620) by Betsy and Giulio Maestro (Mulberry, 1994)

Franklin Watts' Expedition series, for example: *Marco Polo: A Journey Through China* (Franklin Watts, 1998)

The Incredible Journey of Lewis and Clark by Rhoda Blumberg (Beechtree, 1987)

Janice Van Cleave's Geography for Every Kid by Janice Van Cleave (John Wiley & Sons, 1993)

Mapped Out! The Search for Snookums by Carol Baicker-McKee (Gibbs-Smith, 1997)

Mapping the World by Sylvia A. Johnson (Atheneum, 1999)

Maps and Mapping by Barbara Taylor (Kingfisher Books, 1993)

Philip's Atlas of the Oceans by John Pernetta (Sterling Publishing Co., 1977)

Older/Adult:

The Atlas of Experience by Louise van Swaaij and Jean Klare (Bloomsbury, 2000)

Be Expert with Map and Compass: The Orienteering Handbook by Bjorn Kjellstrom (Scribner's, 1955, 1976)

The Dictionary of Imaginary Places, revised edition by Alberto Manguel and Giannin Guadulupi (Harvest, 2000)

The Discoverers: A History of Man's Search to Know His World and Himself by Daniel J. Boorstin (Random House, 1983)

Earth from Above by Yann Arthus-Bertrand (Harry N. Abrams, 1999)

Envisioning Information by Edward R. Tufte (Graphics Press, 1990)

Flattening the Earth: Two Thousand Years of Map Projections by John P. Snyder (University of Chicago Press, 1993)

The Geographical Imagination in America, 1880–1950 by Susan Schulten (Chicago University Press, 2001)

Hidden in Plain View: A Secret Story of Quilts and the Underground Railroad by Jacqueline L. Tobin and Raymond G. Dobard, Ph.D. (Doubleday, 1999)

How to Lie with Maps by Mark S. Monmonier and H.J. DeBlij (University of Chicago Press, 1996)

The Mapmakers, revised edition by John Noble Wilford (Knopf, 2000)

Mapping the Next Millennium by Stephen S. Hall (Random House, 1992)

New Found Lands: Maps in the History of Exploration by Peter Whitfield (Routledge, 1998)

The New Nature of Maps by J.B. Harley (Johns Hopkins Press, 2001)

Parallax: The Race to Measure the Cosmos by Alan W. Hirshfeld (W.H. Freeman, 2001)

The Power of Maps by Denis Wood with John Fels (The Guilford Press, 1992)

The Seekers: The Story of Man's Continuing Quest to Understand His World by Daniel J. Boorstin (Random House, 1999)

Web Cartography by Menno-Jan Kraak and Allan Brown (Taylor and Francis, 2000)

Web Sites

Great Globe Gallery—gobs of gorgeous globes

> http://hum.amu.edu.pl/~zbzw/glob/glob1.htm

Earth Science Image Gallery—the earth from space

> http://www.earth.nasa.gov/gallery/index.html

National Geographic Map Machine—make your own maps

> http://www.nationalgeographic.com/maps/

Mapquest—make your own travel maps

> http://www.mapquest.com

National Oceanic and Atmospheric Administration (NOAA) Central Library—weather and water

> http://www.lib.noaa.gov

National Imagery and Mapping Agency (NIMA)—maps from satellites

> http://www.nima.mil

National Aeronautics and Space Administration (NASA) home page—the U.S. space program

> http://www.nasa.gov

National Space Science Data Center—space mapping

> http://nssdc.gsfc.nasa.gov/planetary/

History of Cartography Project, University of Wisconsin—information about maps

> http://feature.geography.wisc.edu/histcart/

NASA Planetary Photojournal—mapping the solar system

> http://photojournal.jpl.nasa.gov/

Star Child/NASA—all kinds of astronomy and space studies

> http://starchild.gsfc.nasa.gov/

Hubble Space Telescope—views of the universe

> http://resources.stsci.edu

U.S. Geological Survey—the place to go for all kinds of U.S. maps to look at or buy

> http://mapping.usgs.gov/

Color Landform Atlas of the U.S.—more maps!

> http://fermi.jhuapl.edu/states/states.html

Perry Castañeda Library Map Collection—University of Texas
http://www.lib.utexas.edu/Libs/PCL/Map_collection/Map_collection.html

U.S. Library of Congress Map Collections
http://memory.loc.gov/ammem/gmdhtml/gmdhome.html

Solar and Heliospheric Observatory (SOHO)—mapping the sun
http://sohowww.nascom.nasa.gov/

Iris Consortium Home Page—watch earthquakes as they occur
http://www.iris.edu

How Far Is It?—from here to wherever
http://www.indo.com/cgi-bin/dist

Green Maps—see more green maps or make your own
http://www.greenmap.com

Landsat Program—views from satellites
http://geo.arc.nasa.gov/sge/landsat/landsat.html

Aerial Cartographers of America—views from on high
http://www.acaq-net.com

Peter H. Dana's Map Projection Overview—what projections change
http://www.colorado.edu/geography/gcraft/notes/mapproj/mapproj.html

Earthview—views of any point on Earth from the sun or the moon
http://www.fourmilab.ch/earthview/vplanet.html

American Museum of Natural History
http://www.amnh.org

Harvard-Smithsonian Center for Astrophysics
http://cfa-www.harvard.edu/

UCLA Brain Mapping Center
http://www.brainmapping.org

Brainland—more brain mapping
http://www.brainland.com

Internet Mapping Project Map Gallery
http://www.cs.bell-labs.com/who/ches/map/gallery/index.html

Index

Photo Credits